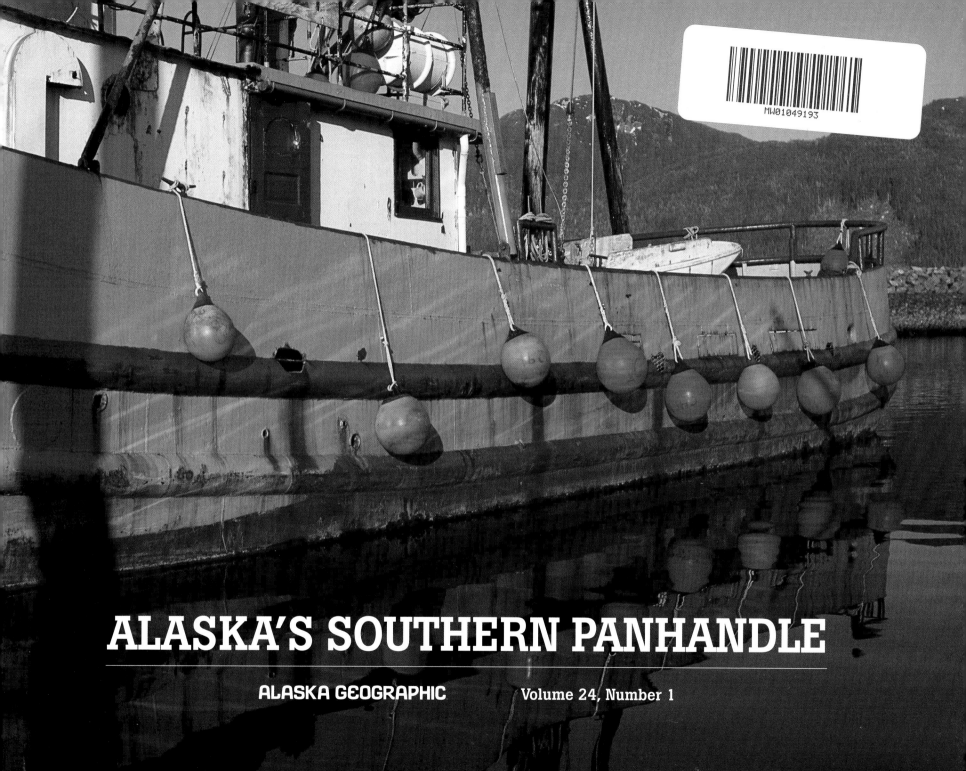

ALASKA'S SOUTHERN PANHANDLE

ALASKA GEOGRAPHIC   Volume 24, Number 1

To teach many more to better know and more wisely use our natural resources...

EDITOR
Penny Rennick

PRODUCTION DIRECTOR
Kathy Doogan

MARKETING MANAGER
Pattey Parker Mancini

CIRCULATION/DATABASE MANAGER
Linda Flowers

EDITORIAL ASSISTANT
Kerre Martineau

BOARD OF DIRECTORS
Richard Carlson
Kathy Doogan
Penny Rennick

Robert A. Henning, **PRESIDENT EMERITUS**

POSTMASTER: Send address changes to:

ALASKA GEOGRAPHIC®
P.O. Box 93370
Anchorage, Alaska 99509-3370

PRINTED IN U.S.A.

ISBN: 1-56661-035-4

Price to non-members this issue: $19.95

COVER: *Small shops line Ketchikan's Creek Street.* (Penny Rennick)

PREVIOUS PAGE: *A fishing boat rides calm waters at Metlakatla.* (Jerry Jordan)

OPPOSITE PAGE: *A floating house is nestled in Traitors Cove off Behm Canal on the west coast of Revillagigedo Island.* (Craig J. Flatten)

ALASKA GEOGRAPHIC® (ISSN 0361-1353) is published quarterly by The Alaska Geographic Society, 639 West International Airport Road, Unit 38, Anchorage, AK 99518. Periodicals postage paid at Anchorage, Alaska, and additional mailing offices. Copyright © 1997 by The Alaska Geographic Society. All rights reserved. Registered trademark: Alaska Geographic, ISSN 0361-1353; Key title Alaska Geographic.

THE ALASKA GEOGRAPHIC SOCIETY is a non-profit, educational organization dedicated to improving geographic understanding of Alaska and the North, putting geography back in the classroom and exploring new methods of teaching and learning.

MEMBERS RECEIVE *ALASKA GEOGRAPHIC®*, a high-quality, colorful quarterly that devotes each issue to monographic, in-depth coverage of a northern region or resource-oriented subject. Back issues are also available. For current membership rates, or to order or request a free catalog of back issues, contact: The Alaska Geographic Society, P.O. Box 93370, Anchorage, AK 99509-3370; phone (907) 562-0164, fax (907) 562-0479, e-mail: akgeo@aol.com

SUBMITTING PHOTOGRAPHS: Those interested in submitting photographs should write for a list of future topics or other specific photo needs and a copy of our editorial guidelines. We cannot be responsible for unsolicited submissions. Submissions not accompanied by sufficient postage for return by certified mail will be returned by regular mail.

CHANGE OF ADDRESS: The post office does not automatically forward *ALASKA GEOGRAPHIC®* when you move. To ensure continuous service, please notify us at least six weeks before moving. Send your new address and membership number or a mailing label from a recent *ALASKA GEOGRAPHIC®* to: Alaska Geographic Society, Box 93370, Anchorage, AK 99509. If your book is returned to us by the post office, we will contact you to ask if you wish to receive a replacement for $5 (to cover postage costs).

COLOR SEPARATIONS: Graphic Chromatics

PRINTING: Hart Press

The Library of Congress has cataloged this serial publication as follows:

Alaska Geographic. v.1-
[Anchorage, Alaska Geographic Society] 1972-
v. ill. (part col.). 23 x 31 cm.
Quarterly
Official publication of The Alaska Geographic Society.
Key title: Alaska geographic, ISSN 0361-1353.

1. Alaska—Description and travel—1959-
—Periodicals. I. Alaska Geographic Society.

F901.A266   917.98'04'505   72-92087

Library of Congress 75[79112] MARC-S.

ABOUT THIS ISSUE: To produce this issue on Ketchikan, Alaska's "First City," and the southern third of the state's panhandle, *ALASKA GEOGRAPHIC®* called on longtime residents of the area Patricia Roppel, Jeanne Gerulskis, Jim Baichtal and Terry Fifield to write articles on the geology, history and lifestyle of the area. *ALASKA GEOGRAPHIC®* staff Penny Rennick and Kerre Martineau wrote the remaining articles.

We thank many residents of southern Southeast for supplying information and insight into the region. In addition to Jim Baichtal and Terry Fifield, residents of Prince of Wales Island, we are indebted to Sharon Brosamle and Diane Stittgen, of Craig and Thorne Bay respectively, for talking with us about their home island. For information on Hyder, we called on Caroline Gutierrez, Ron Thomas and postmaster Ed Dolsky. Marti Miller of the U.S. Geological Survey provided information on the geology of Hyder. Laura Burns, staff member of Misty Fiords National Monument, U. S. Forest Service, outlined management plans for the forested areas around Hyder. Leroy Coon and Steven Bradford of the state Department of Transportation and Public Facilities provided information on the bridges of the Salmon River drainage near Hyder, and Bill Wright of the state Department of Education clarified the educational arrangements for Hyder students. Bob DeArmond, longtime dean of Southeast historians, provided details of Hyder's history, including the correct name of the man for whom the town is named. Mary C. Nicolson of the Alaska Newspaper Project, Alaska State Library, dug out references to early Hyder newspapers. Finally, we thank Bruce Merrell and Dan Fleming of the Z.J. Loussac Library in Anchorage for suggesting topics and providing information on many aspects of southern Southeast. ∎

Contents

Alaska's Southern Panhandle

By Penny Rennick

Southeast Alaska clings to the mountainous Pacific coast and reaches southeastward toward Canada's British Columbia and the U.S.'s Pacific Northwest. The region, frequently called the Panhandle, consists of a sliver of mainland and a multitude of islands contained within the Alexander Archipelago. Southern Southeast is that portion of the Panhandle south of the mainland's Cleveland Peninsula and all islands south of the northern tip of Prince of Wales Island. The region's population and commerce center on Ketchikan, connected to the rest of the state and Outside by commercial jet service and by ferry service via the Alaska Marine Highway System. Satellite communities dot the bays of Prince of Wales and Annette islands. Tiny settlements, sometimes consisting of no more than one or two families, are tucked away amid quiet coves off the region's plentiful waterways. The only exception to this marine network is isolated Hyder, a one-of-a-kind outpost at the short end of the Alaska-Yukon Highway. And even Hyder receives ferry service every other week in summer.

Several issues confront the residents of southern Southeast. The timber industry, long a mainstay of the region's economy, has been buffeted by economical, political and philosophical debate. The fishing industry faces increasing rancor from Canadian counterparts over which fish belong to which fishermen. The region's water transportation network, based on the Alaska Marine Highway System's ferries, is undergoing a thorough review to expand service. And tourism is taking over as the region's most potent economic force.

Southern Southeast's citizens have always been resourceful and flexible. They live in a rich region. Early Native inhabitants found it so, as do today's residents. With far-sighted thinking, the bounty of their homeland can be balanced to provide well for residents and visitors of the next century. ∎

FACING PAGE: *A temperate rain forest of Sitka spruce (shown here) and western hemlock covers much of Alaska's southern Panhandle. As early as 1902, part of this forest was encompassed within the Alexander Archipelago Forest Reserve. By 1908, this reserve and additional forested lands were combined into the Tongass National Forest. (Jerry Jordan)*

The Geological, Glacial and Cultural History of Southern Southeast

By Jim Baichtal, Greg Streveler and Terence Fifield

EDITOR'S NOTE: *Jim is a geologist with the U.S. Forest Service in Thorne Bay, Greg is a geological and environmental consultant from Gustavus and Terence is an archaeologist with the U.S. Forest Service in Craig.*

I n 1879, while traveling through Southeast Alaska's Alexander Archipelago, John Muir wrote, "The variety we find, as to the contours and the collocation of the islands, is due chiefly to the differences in the structure and composition of their rocks, and the unequal glacial denudation different portions of the coast were subjected to." Muir's observations hold true. Much of what observers see in the landforms and biological communities is controlled by the geology and the area's subsequent glacial history.

The geology and geomorphology of southern Southeast Alaska are extremely complex. The region is situated at the end of a plate tectonics conveyor belt that has piled fragmented pieces of extinct continents into its shores, building a geologically diverse region. Many different fragments, or terranes, have combined to form the land. This complex geology has been overprinted and modified by the glacial events of the distant and recent past, leaving the present landforms. Post-glacial isostatic rebound, sea-level fluctuations and tectonic uplift and/or down-warping has added further variety to the landscape. Geology is a major delineator for much of the geomorphology and landforms. So little time has passed since deglaciation, some 10,000 to 14,000 years, that little soil has developed from the weathering of the bedrock. In most areas, only the initial and/or reworked glacial deposits mask the bedrock. Wetlands or peatlands have developed on top of the poorly drained areas and dense forests inhabit the more productive, better-drained sites. Because southern Southeast is so geologically young and because soil development is so limited, geology plays a major role in species distribution, diversity and isolation of individuals.

FACING PAGE: *Kayaking is ideal for those who want to slowly take in the beauty of Misty Fiords National Monument. This kayak, beached near the mouth of Grace Creek off the west side of Behm Canal, is loaded with gear for a week long-trip through the 2.3-million-acre national monument. (George Matz)*

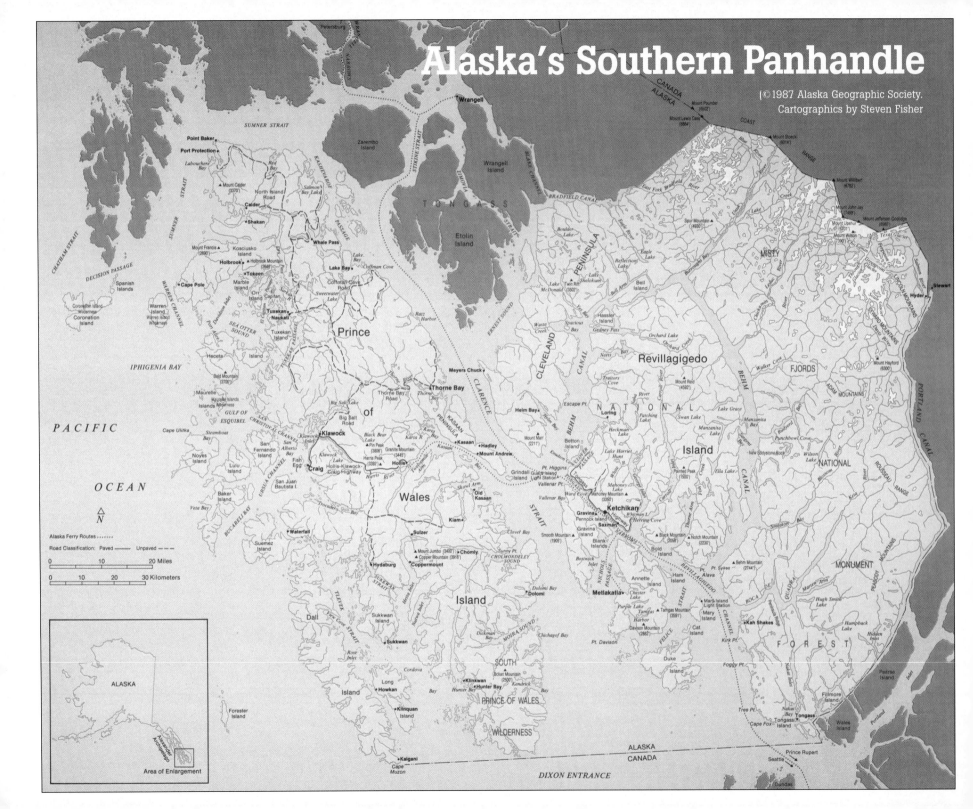

Alaska's Southern Panhandle

©1987 Alaska Geographic Society.
Cartographics by Steven Fisher

Unraveling the Puzzle:
Geologic History of Southern Southeast

A founding principle of geology is that rocks carry history in their chemistry, mineralogy and relationship to each other. Reading these clues, geologists long ago figured out a story line for parts of the world with relatively simple geology, usually in continental interiors. Continental margins turned out to be harder and Southeast's margin certainly was no exception.

Serious study of the southern Alexander Archipelago's geology began about 70 years ago, but for decades the standard geological approach led more to confusion than clarity. A rock unit was often found to be contorted and shattered, ending abruptly in most directions, to be replaced by rocks seemingly unrelated to it. Four-hundred-million-year-old coral reef limestones might end at a shatter zone, where 200-million-year-old sediments of an entirely different origin might abruptly begin. In another direction, rocks with chemistry suggesting shallow burial might be interrupted by, say, a body of highly altered rocks that were deeply buried at one time in their history. Southern Southeast's geological map, the product of lots of careful work, was a real mess that seemed to say little of coherence about the area's history.

Chaos reigned in geologists' interpretations until the last couple of decades, when progress began to be made as a result of a new way of looking at the earth's surface called "crustal plate theory." According to this theory, the earth's crust consists of discrete plates afloat on a semiliquid mantle. The crustal plates drift relative to each other in response to the mantle's currents. Where the plates meet, there is always great geological activity, generating the lion's share of the world's mountain ranges, oceanic trenches, volcanoes and earthquakes. Many of these boundaries are at the edges of continents. Southeast Alaska turns out to lie along the seam between the North American and Pacific crustal plates.

Several things can happen where two plates meet. If the plates are converging, rocks of one may plunge under the other, ride up and over, or be compressed and folded into a thick mass. Plates may diverge, creating a void into which the mantle wells

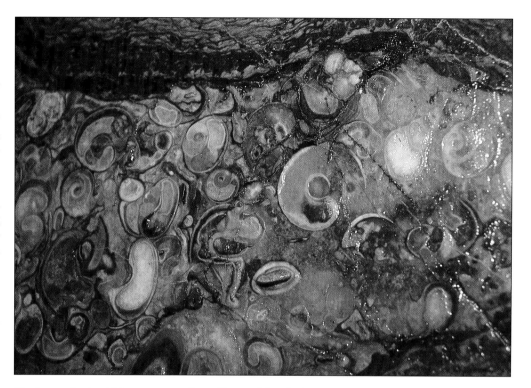

Photographed within a cave wall on Heceta Island, these gastropods and brachiopods are packed into the open area between stromatolites, a form of calcereous algae. The rock is fossiliferous limestone of the Silurian-aged Heceta Formation, characterized by pure carbonate rocks that originated as marine reef and lagoonal deposits near the equator some 438 to 408 million years ago. These deposits were rafted atop spreading oceanic plates until they docked on the ancient shores of Southeast. (Jim Baichtal, courtesy of the U.S. Forest Service)

up to form new crustal material. Or plates may chafe past each other. Sometimes smaller blocks of crust break off and get battered along plate edges until they settle down and become welded to another piece.

When geologists applied crustal plate theory to southern Southeast's situation, things finally began to make sense. During the Age of Dinosaurs, North America began to diverge from

Europe, giving birth to the Atlantic Ocean. As the Atlantic rift widened, the North American crustal plate moved slowly westward away from Europe, overriding the Pacific plate. Meanwhile, the Pacific plate had been gradually rotating in a counterclockwise direction. Some thicker pieces of the Pacific plate occasionally refused to be overridden; instead they shattered and smeared along the plate edge, sometimes welding on to become a part of North America. Other pieces have come along and welded onto the outer edge of the earlier ones. At the latitude of southern Southeast, this accretionary process has been going on for perhaps 170 million years. It is going on right now. Southern Southeast Alaska's patchwork geology is the result.

So, according to this new way of looking at earth's history, southern Southeast really is not a bona fide part of North America at all, but a conglomeration of fragments crumbled off other crustal plates and smeared onto the continent's edge. Geologists call these fragments terranes.

LEFT: *Folded sediments along the road between Craig and Klawock on Prince of Wales Island contain Mississippian-age, thin-bedded, gray-black chert, cut by an igneous dike. (Mark Fritzke, courtesy of the U.S. Forest Service)*

BELOW: *This obsidian tuff comes from Cape Felix on Suemez Island. By 9,000 years ago people were using obsidian, and evidence of this use has been recovered from the Ground Hog Bay site in northern Southeast. Widespread use of obsidian has been cited as support for the theory of a well-developed trade network among prehistoric people in Southeast. (Jim Baichtal, courtesy of the U.S. Forest Service)*

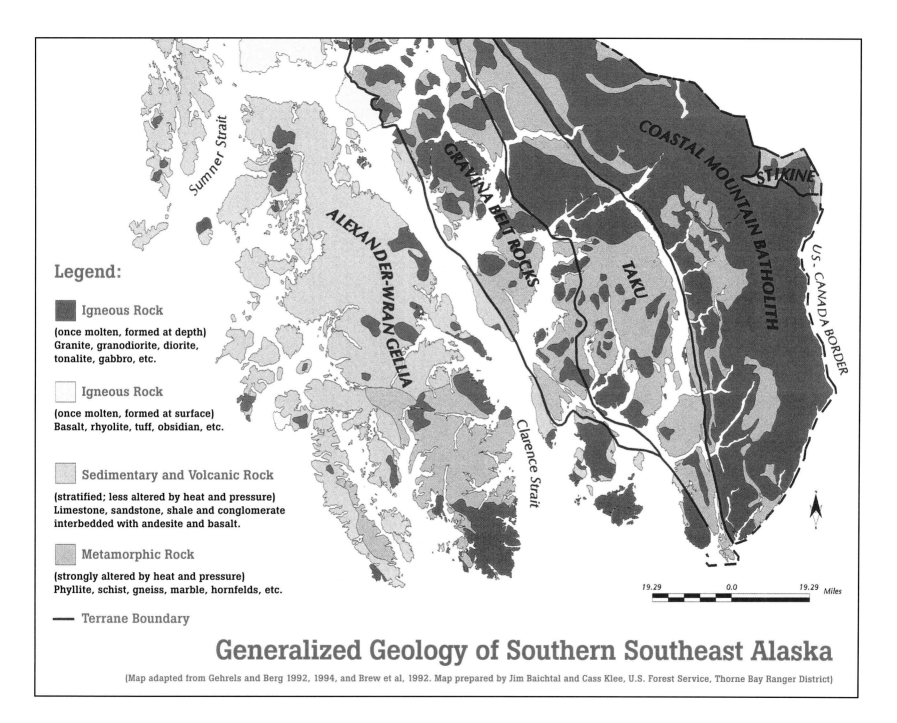

Legend:

■ **Igneous Rock**

(once molten, formed at depth)
Granite, granodiorite, diorite,
tonalite, gabbro, etc.

□ **Igneous Rock**

(once molten, formed at surface)
Basalt, rhyolite, tuff, obsidian, etc.

▢ **Sedimentary and Volcanic Rock**

(stratified; less altered by heat and pressure)
Limestone, sandstone, shale and conglomerate
interbedded with andesite and basalt.

▨ **Metamorphic Rock**

(strongly altered by heat and pressure)
Phyllite, schist, gneiss, marble, hornfelds, etc.

— **Terrane Boundary**

Sumner Strait

ALEXANDER-WRAN GELLIA

GRAVINA BELT ROCKS

COASTAL MOUNTAIN BATHOLITH

STIKINE

TAKU

Clarence Strait

US - CANADA BORDER

19.29   0.0   19.29 *Miles*

Generalized Geology of Southern Southeast Alaska

(Map adapted from Gehrels and Berg 1992, 1994, and Brew et al, 1992. Map prepared by Jim Baichtal and Cass Klee, U.S. Forest Service, Thorne Bay Ranger District)

The tranquillity of Blue Lake in this view looking east toward the Coast Mountains and Canada offers no hint of the lake's turbulent beginning during a volcanic eruption a little more than a century ago. (Jim Battle, courtesy of U.S. Forest Service)

The details of southern Southeast's construction are still debated. Not all geologists agree on the sequence of accretions, or on the resultant terrane boundaries. Taking all this into account, the general picture is something like this: Before the Atlantic rift formed, the west coast of North America lay in what is now Western Canada and southern Southeast did not exist. By 100 million years ago, several terranes had welded on, their western edge extending into what is now the Coast Mountains and Portland Canal.

Meanwhile, an offshore large island group that had originated in the tropics was moving northward astride the Pacific plate; geologists would come to call the rocks comprising it the Alexander Terrane. This island group had a spine of ancient volcanic rocks fringed by limestone reefs and muddy sea bottom sediments. During the journey northward, it had been injected with younger volcanic deposits as it passed over a hot spot in the earth's interior; these volcanics and related sediments came to be called the Wrangellia Terrane. As Alexander/Wrangellia was compressed by the strains of an approaching North America, it developed a major surface wrinkle into which sediments were shed; those sediments are called the Gravina Belt.

Sometime before the last dinosaurs were exterminated, Alexander/Wrangellia/Gravina began to collide with North America. The intense pressures buckled parts of the collision zone downward, several miles deep into the earth, where they became cooked and interjected with liquid granite from below. By contrast, rocks on the terranes' trailing edge were far enough from the collision to be less affected, barely altered enough to change their mineral composition.

Meanwhile, North America continued moving inexorably into the Pacific. The leading portion of Alexander/Wrangellia/Gravina, now welded onto the continent, moved with it. The outer portion was still attached to the Pacific plate, which was rotating northward. Something had to give. Cracks developed, allowing rocks from the west to slip northward. As the collision progressed, cracks developed farther to the west and old eastern ones tended to weld shut, but they remained as weakness zones later gouged by glacial activity into major fiords like Behm Canal and Clarence Strait. Today, the main active crack, called the Queen Charlotte fault, lies offshore near the present edge of the continental shelf.

As the action moved westward, pressure on the eastern zone was relieved. Rocks forced deep into the earth now rebounded strongly to form the Coast Mountains. Rocks less deeply downthrown and thus under less strain were upthrust more gently, and the Revillagigedo/Prince of Wales Island area came to be.

Farthest to the west, northern Prince of Wales and the

associated outer islands were formed from rocks affected relatively little by the great events of their arrival along North America. Prince of Wales Island lies just east of the active seam between the Pacific and North America plates, the Fairweather-Queen Charlotte fault. This places the outer coast of Prince of Wales in the line of fire for the next great accretive event, whenever that should occur.

If one traveled west to east across Prince of Wales Island, across Gravina Island through Ketchikan and on eastward to the Alaska-Canada boundary, one would cross up to five terrane blocks, depending on which theory held sway. Each terrane has a suite of rock types within it that spans a range of geologic ages. The following is a brief description of the dominant rock types that would occur within each terrane.

Alexander-Wrangellia Terranes

Prince of Wales and the surrounding islands are made up solely of the Alexander Terrane. Duke Island, most of Annette Island, the western half of Gravina Island and the tip of Cleveland Peninsula are composed of the Alexander-Wrangellia terranes. These terranes are made of a variety of stratified, metamorphic and plutonic rocks of latest Precambrian to Cambrian through Middle Jurassic age, about 570 million to 170 million years ago. The youngest rocks crop out in a fairly narrow belt along the eastern margin of the terrane. Shallow marine sediments such as limestone and mudstone, sandstone, and conglomerate derived from volcanic sediments of Silurian age (440 to 408 million years ago) are the most widespread units in

The remains of trees burnt off by a lava flow can still be seen in the surface of the Blue River Lava Flow in Misty Fiords National Monument. The lava erupted from a vent just across the United States-Canada boundary. In the late 1800s, basaltic lava flowed from this vent 12 miles to temporarily dam the Unuk River. In the early 1900s, the expedition mapping the Alaska-Canada boundary found the nearly fresh lava an imposing obstacle to cross. (Jim Baichtal, courtesy of the U.S. Forest Service)

FACING PAGE: *Subalpine fir are commonly found within areas of karst development on top of limestone-capped peaks on Prince of Wales and surrounding islands. Some researchers have suggested that the presence of this fir could indicate areas that were not glaciated during the height of the Wisconsin glaciation. (Jim Baichtal, courtesy of U.S. Forest Service)*

RIGHT: *Highly sheared and fractured Heceta Limestone characterizes the alpine reaches of some Southeast islands. Many of the fractures are more than 100 feet deep. (Jim Battle, courtesy of U.S. Forest Service)*

LOWER RIGHT: *Chemicals leaching through the pure limestone after heavy rainfall have created this intense karst development on Dall Island. Within this environment are deep caves that harbor fossils providing clues to prehistoric southern Southeast. (Mark Fritzke, courtesy of the U.S. Forest Service)*

the terrane. It is within the carbonates of this terrane that extensive karst and cave systems have developed. Generally, rocks of the north half of Prince of Wales Island show little regional metamorphism and are only slightly deformed. Rocks of southern Prince of Wales Island are highly metamorphosed and deformed. Locally, the Alexander-Wrangellia terranes are intruded by late Cretaceous (145 to 65 million years ago) granodiorite plutons.

Gravina Belt Rocks

Northern Annette, eastern Gravina, the western fourth of Revillagigedo Island, and most of central Cleveland Peninsula are underlain by Gravina Belt rocks. These rocks were deposited on top of the Alexander-Wrangellia terranes. The Gravina Belt rocks are composed of stratified and plutonic rocks of Upper Jurassic to mid-Cretaceous age, about 208 to 100 million years ago. Marine sandstone and mudstone, graywacke and inter-bedded volcanic rocks intruded by a variety of plutons are the most common rock types encountered.

Tightly folded, interbedded calcareous mudstone and shale on the outer coast of Baker Island southwest of Craig provide evidence of the tortured geologic history of the Alexander Terrane. (Jim Baichtal, courtesy of U.S. Forest Service)

Taku Terrane

Moving farther east, the southern mainland, eastern three quarters of Revillagigedo Island and the remaining portion of Cleveland Peninsula are composed of rocks variously interpreted as those of a unique terrane (Taku) or a highly scrambled mixture of Alexander/Wrangellia/Gravina fragments. All of Ketchikan is developed within this terrane. The terrane is a poorly understood assemblage of deformed and metamorphosed strata of Early Permian to mid-Cretaceous age, about 270 to 100 million years ago. Phyllite, schist, minor marble and metavolcanic rocks intruded by Cretaceous-aged granodiorite and tonalite plutons are the most common rock types present.

Coastal Mountain Batholith Complex or Cache Creek Terrane

The lands east of Behm Canal mainly belong to the Coastal Mountains Batholith Complex or Cache Creek Terrane. This terrane contains the granite that is the foundation of Misty Fiords National Monument. This terrane is composed chiefly of Early Cretaceous to Paleocene granodiorite and tonalite plutonic rocks 54 to 135 million years old. Approximately 20 percent of the terrane is composed of metasedimentary and metavolcanic schist and gneiss.

Stikine Terrane

Finally, a relatively small area west and north of Hyder is characterized by Devonian to Middle Jurassic (408 to 180 million years ago) carbonate, volcanic, sedimentary rocks intruded by Eocene granodiorite and quartz monzonite plutons.

At times molten rock has followed the deep fractures formed along and within the terrane boundaries. This molten rock has spewed onto the earth's surface forming the basalt/andesite/rhyolite, and obsidian of Suemez Island off the western coast of Prince of Wales Island. Other recent volcanic events are evidenced by the welded ash of Painted Peak and the basalt of Princess Bay on Revillagigedo Island, New Eddystone Rock, and the basalt of Punchbowl and Checats coves within Misty Fiords National Monument. The most recent volcanism in southern

Southeast sent basaltic lavas flowing down the valley floor of the Blue River in Misty Fiords National Monument. Erupting some 360 years ago and again in the late 1890s from a vent just inside Canada, the lava flowed some 12 miles creating the basin for Blue Lake and terminating in the Unuk River where it formed the restriction known as First Canyon. In the early 1900s, the expedition mapping the Alaska-Canada boundary found the nearly fresh surface of the lava a challenge to traverse.

Glacial History of Southern Southeast

As the Coast Mountains were forced higher, the range that formed began to intercept the onshore airflow from the Pacific. This warm, ocean air carried with it abundant moisture that fell as rain and snow as it tried to rise over the newly formed range. Snows began to accumulate on the uplands and form glacial ice. During the last several million years, glaciers have expanded and invaded the lowlands as the climate periodically cooled.

Because of the dynamic geologic and glacial past of the southern archipelago, there is a long gap in the record of events on the land. Before the Pleistocene, the latest evidence of life is the Cretaceous-aged rocks of the Gravina Belt. Fossils from these rocks give scientists a glimpse of life in the sea some 100 million years ago. Some 6 million years ago the volcano that gave rise to New Eddystone Rock erupted. The basalt that filled a valley near Punchbowl Lake in Misty Fiords erupted some 400,000 years ago. Glacial deposits on top of some of the highest peaks on Prince of Wales Island may hold some clues but have not yet yielded datable material. The oldest fossil remains from the Pleistocene in southern Southeast are those of a marmot from a small cave on northern Prince of Wales that has dated to more than 45,000 years before present.

During the last 2 million years of the Pleistocene, glaciers have sculpted the Alexander Archipelago many times. Scientists do not know how often glaciers have invaded the land; subsequent glacial advances have destroyed much of the evidence of earlier advances. The rounded mountains, ridges and low hills, the broad U-shaped valleys, the deep fiords and

As the glaciers melted, icebergs that calved from glacial fronts filled many of the bays or became isolated along shorelines. Here they melted, dropping the sediments they contained. Included in the sediments were large boulders known as glacial erratics, which today mark historical shorelines. The glacial erratics shown here litter muskeg hundreds of feet above and away from the present sea's edge. (Greg Streveler)

LEFT: *Wooden weir stakes from prehistoric fish traps suggest subsistence styles of the early inhabitants of Southeast. The earliest remains of such fish traps are found within the eroding banks of rivers and streams far up from their current mouths. As the land rebounded after deglaciation, old weirs were abandoned and subsequently buried. This stake came from the banks of the Thorne River on Prince of Wales Island and dates to some 3,800 years ago. The stake was preserved in muds originally laid down in an estuary. (Jim Baichtal, courtesy of U.S. Forest Service)*

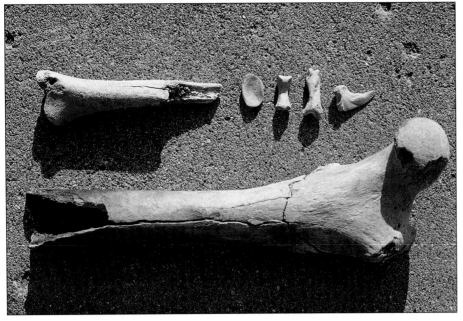

LOWER LEFT: *These bones were recovered from near surface sediments from a cave on northern Prince of Wales Island. The upper bone is from a black bear and has been dated to 41,600 years ago. The large, lower bone is from a brown bear that has been dated to 35,363 years ago. The Pleistocene paleontology of the area is primarily known from cave and rock shelter deposits, which are often intimately related to archaeological sites. The cool, stable, basic environments in the caves result in exceptionally good preservation of bone and organic materials. Recent paleontological work in caves on Prince of Wales and surrounding islands, along with botanical surveys of alpine areas and genetic studies on brown bear and salmon populations, argue for a well-developed coastal refugium along the western coast of Southeast. (Dr. Tim Heaton, courtesy of U.S. Forest Service)*

FACING PAGE: *This aerial shows typical glacial geomorphology within the Coastal Mountain Batholith Complex of Misty Fiords National Monument. The view is looking toward Behm Canal across Manzoni Lake. (U.S. Forest Service)*

thick deposits of glacial sediments all attest to the repeated attack of the glaciers.

The glacial history of the southern Alexander Archipelago has been the subject of much speculation. As recently as 1990, it was thought that all but the peaks that rose above 3,000 feet were ice covered during the height of the last Great Ice Age.

Research within the caves on Prince of Wales and surrounding islands, analysis of sediments within basins and offshore of the Queen Charlotte Islands, and genetic studies of island populations within the archipelago have shed light on the glacial history of southern Southeast.

By about 70,000 years ago, the last Great Ice Age had begun. It is known to researchers as the Wisconsin Glacial Stage, or simply the Wisconsin. The Wisconsin ended about 10,000 years ago. People tend to think of a great wall of ice

This skull and bones of a black bear were discovered in El Capitan Cave on northern Prince of Wales Island. The bones, stained by tannin in surface waters that leaked through from the forest floor above, have been dated to 10,745 years ago. The remains of five black bears have been dated, suggesting that this species has inhabited Southeast from at least 41,600 years ago to the present. (R. Carlson, courtesy of U.S. Forest Service)

advancing across the land when in fact the glacial periods were a composite of glacial advances and retreats, of valley and alpine glaciers that repeatedly grew, advanced and coalesced to form thick ice sheets that covered all but the highest peaks. An intervening warm period, the middle Wisconsin interstadial, was characterized by temperatures only slightly cooler than today in which glaciers receded more than advanced. The middle Wisconsin interstadial ended from 27,000 to 25,000 years ago and the glaciers of the late Wisconsin began their advance. These were the most recent glaciers to cover most of southern Southeast. The extent of these glaciers is clearly evident in the shape and form of the land today.

Researchers can only guess at the exact extent of ice during early advances of the early and middle Wisconsin, for the latest advance has erased most of the evidence left by the previous ones. From the sediments within several small caves on north Prince of Wales Island, researchers do get a brief look at the fauna and flora of the interstadial period. Bones of brown bear, three black bears and two marmots have been recovered. These bones dated to between 44,500 and 28,700 years old. Pollen of alder, spruce, birch, juniper and sedge were recovered from sediments surrounding a black bear tibia bone dating to 41,000 years before present. These finds suggest a climate and vegetation much different from that found throughout the region today.

The late Wisconsin glaciers that began their advance 27,000 to 25,000 years ago reached their maximum extent before 16,000 to 14,000 years ago. Sea levels were as much as 390 feet lower worldwide during the late Wisconsin maximum because so much water was tied up in glacial ice. This lowering of the sea level probably created vast lowlands on the continental shelf to the west of Prince of Wales and narrowed or eliminated waterways among the islands seen today. Many of these islands would have been connected by land. In places, ice sheets and valley glaciers flowed onto the lowlands. Open areas may have existed between the glaciers in which plants, animals and possibly humans could have lived. These areas are known as glacial refugia. Fossil ringed seal bones from caves on Prince of Wales dating from 20,700 to 13,700 years ago suggest that pack ice may have been forming off the southern Southeast coastline.

By the end of the late Wisconsin glacial advance, this landscape had undergone dramatic changes. From central Prince of Wales Island eastward, the region looked a lot like Greenland, a single vast plateau of ice with glaciers descending to the sea. Ice more than a mile thick covered the valleys of Misty Fiords, tapering to some 3,000 feet in the vicinity of Ketchikan. From the Alaska–Canada boundary westward to the spine of Prince of Wales Island, only the highest peaks, known as nunataks, rose above the ice. Ice sheets flowed across northern, central and eastern Prince of Wales, coalescing with alpine glaciers of the Klawock Mountains and southern Prince of Wales and Dall islands. Glaciers moved westward around northern Prince of Wales through El Capitan Passage, across Sea Otter Sound, down Black Bear Creek and across Big Salt, through the Harris and Klawock river drainages. Ice flowed through to Trocadero Bay and past Hydaburg. At this time, valley glaciers filled the many fiords of Dall Island. Scientists do not yet know how far west the ice extended onto the lowlands created by the lowering of the sea levels. Research is now being focused on answering these questions.

As early as 14,000 to 16,000 years ago the glaciers of the late Wisconsin began their retreat. The deep ice that had once covered the area had receded back beyond Ketchikan, as is evidenced by fossil shells more than 12,000 years old in deposits in the downtown area. Similar evidence suggests that not only Ketchikan but Petersburg and Juneau were ice-free by this time as well. The landscape that emerged from under the glaciers was different from what is visible today. The soils formed before the last glacial advance had been scoured away and only newly deposited glacial sediments remained. In transforming the landscape, the glaciers had deepened and sculpted the valleys into broad U-shapes and rounded the ridge crests. Under a new set of climatic conditions, plants began to recolonize the land. The first plants most likely came from scattered refugia throughout southern Southeast. Researchers

As the late Wisconsin glaciers grew, the landscapes of Southeast became dominated by ice. From central Prince of Wales Island eastward, the region looked a lot like Greenland, a single vast plateau of ice with glaciers descending to the sea. Ice more than a mile thick covered the valleys of Misty Fiords, tapering to some 3,000 feet in the vicinity of Ketchikan. The valleys of western Prince of Wales may have looked much like the glaciers found today throughout Glacier Bay National Park. (U.S. Forest Service)

have not yet found evidence of what vegetation existed after deglaciation. However, lake sediments from near Gustavus in northern Southeast contain pollen that indicates tundra vegetation existed until about 12,000 years ago. These same lake sediments suggest a change to a milder, warmer and damper climate at this time. Pine and mountain hemlock became established. These combined with alder and willow to dominate until 10,500 years ago when the climate became cooler and

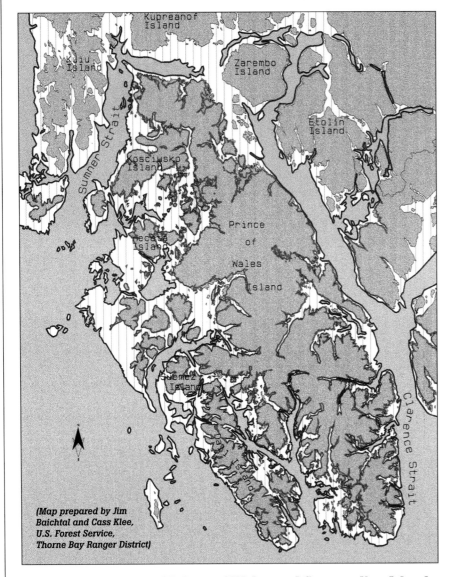

Ancient Shorelines of Prince of Wales and Surrounding Islands

—— Present Shoreline

—— Late Pleistocene Shoreline: 11,000 to 16,000 years ago the shoreline was at or below this line, which represents the -300 foot contour. This occurred during the maximum extent of the Late Wisconsin Glaciation. Major lakes and basins are also shown.

—— Possible Holocene Shoreline: based on consistent occurrence of raised marine deposits at 50 feet in elevation or less; dating between 8,500 and 9,500 years before present.

(Map prepared by Jim Baichtal and Cass Klee, U.S. Forest Service, Thorne Bay Ranger District)

drier, and tundra vegetation returned. These conditions lasted for 500 years until the climate did an abrupt change, bringing about conditions drier and warmer than today. Ice may have even receded back farther than is found today. By 9,000 to 8,000 years ago, spruce-hemlock forests dominated the landscape and by 6,000 to 5,000 years ago peat bogs were forming.

From the remains of mammals discovered in the caves of Prince of Wales and the surrounding islands, scientists have evidence of some of the fauna present between 13,000 and 9,000 years ago. Many of the species found no longer inhabit Prince of Wales. These include extant species such as brown bear, caribou, red fox, wolverine, heather vole, lemming and possibly mountain goat. Except for caribou, all species can be found on the adjacent mainland today. Caribou existed on the Queen Charlotte Islands until historic times. Why certain species disappeared from the islands of the southern archipelago after deglaciation is uncertain. Besides the mainland, brown bears today inhabit Admiralty, Chichagof and Baranof islands to the north. Brown bears are the only bear found on these islands. Today, brown bears and black bears do not inhabit the same islands of the archipelago. Why brown bears and black bears coexisted on Prince of Wales Island, even inhabiting the same caves until at least 7,200 years ago is not understood. It is not known either why or when brown bears disappeared from Prince of Wales Island. Researchers do know from local Native oral traditions and the mammal bones found in caves that both early humans and brown bears coexisted on Prince of Wales Island. These discoveries also suggest that these animals were trapped here by advancing ice and that they survived in habitable coastal refugia, a refugia that may have been home to a variety of animals and man. One can imagine a post-glacial, tundra-dominated landscape inhabited by animals and resembling the coastal tundra bordering the Bering Sea today.

As previously mentioned, the fringes of the great ice sheet had begun to retreat between 16,000 and 14,000 years ago. Beginning 12,000 to 11,000 years ago, the thick ice caps started to melt in earnest. Remember too that the land surface was depressed by the weight of the glacial ice. The land began to

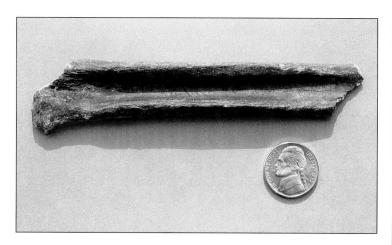

ABOVE: *A cave on northern Prince of Wales Island yielded this caribou bone, which dated to 10,515 years ago. Caribou no longer inhabit Southeast. Caribou did however exist on the Queen Charlotte Islands until historical times. Many of the animal species found within the caves no longer inhabit Prince of Wales Island. These include extant species such as brown bear, red fox, wolverine, heather vole, lemming and possibly mountain goat. Why certain species disappeared from the islands of the southern Alexander Archipelago after deglaciation is uncertain. (Dr. Tim Heaton, courtesy of U.S. Forest Service)*

RIGHT: *This chert biface or spear point was recovered from a cave on northern Prince of Wales Island. The remains of a human dated to 9,800 years ago were recently discovered nearby. It is not known if the point is associated with the remains. (Jim Baichtal, courtesy of U.S. Forest Service)*

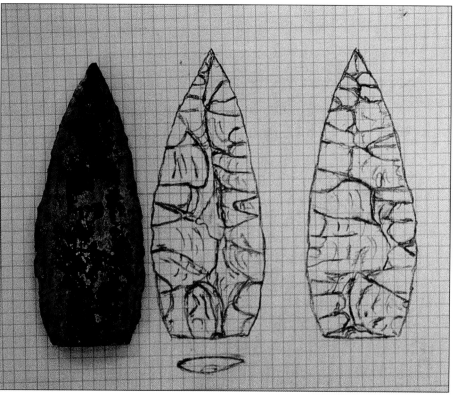

rebound once the glaciers had retreated; however, the sea reinvaded the land faster than the earth's crust rebounded. This resulted in the sea rising, covering lands that are now above sea level.

From 11,000 to 9,500 years ago, sea level may have risen as much as 2.5 inches per year. Think about the effects of such a rapid rise in sea level. The western portion of southern Southeast became a drowned landscape with many islands and inlets. The islands were separated by more water than they are today. The sea filled valleys and inundated the broad areas of coastal tundra on which animals and early man might have lived. During this time, sea level would have risen 2 feet every 10 years, 20 feet every century. Think about the effects such a rapid change in sea level would have on the communities of Southeast today. Between 9,500 and 8,500 years ago, sea level reached its maximum height. Eventually, the rebounding land caught up with the invading sea. By approximately 6,000 years ago, the shorelines of western Prince of Wales Island had adjusted from their highest point to near current levels. This is an average model, one not applicable to lands east of Prince of Wales and surrounding islands.

With the melting of the glaciers, icebergs filled many of the bays or became isolated along shorelines. Here they melted, dropping the sediment they contained. Included in the sediments were large boulders known as glacial erratics. Today, lines of boulders or erratics mark historic shorelines. Sediments laid down in near shore environments rose above the stabilizing sea level. How far above depended on the amount of rebound. Glacial marine sediments, some bearing fossils, erratics and erosional features are found today at or above present sea level. These attest to the amount of rebound and infer the thickness of overriding ice, i.e. the greater the ice thickness, the greater the rebound. Moving west to east across southern Southeast, geologists find such deposits at the following elevations: 1) On western Prince of Wales Island, glacial marine sediments and erratics are found from present sea level to 20 to 50 feet elevation. Such deposits have been found at similar elevations on eastern Prince of Wales. 2) In the vicinity of Gravina Island and Ketchikan, glacial marine shell deposits exist from 80 to 100 feet. 3) Just to the east of Revillagigedo Island, within Behm Canal, is 237-foot-tall New Eddystone Rock, which is the core of a volcanic cone that has been eroded as the land rebounded after deglaciation. As the land rose and waves eroded all but the most resistant rock, geologists were left with a measure of the amount of rebound at this site. 4) Glacial marine sediments are found along Portland Canal to its head at a minimum elevation of 340 feet and possibly as high as 500 feet.

The timing of the retreat of the glaciers from the valleys of

LEFT: *A stratigraphic profile at the site where the Thorne River basket was found shows the fine-grained, water-saturated silts that formed the air-tight vault protecting the basket. Above the gray silts is a thin layer of gravel overlain by repeating flood deposits, evidence of the gradual uplift of the land. (Terence Fifield, courtesy of U.S. Forest Service)*

BELOW: *This small segment of a 5,360-year-old spruce root basket was recovered from the lower Thorne River in 1994. The basket was cylindrical, measuring approximately 7 inches in diameter and 13 inches tall. (Jim Peterson, University of Maine, Farmington, courtesy of Terence Fifield)*

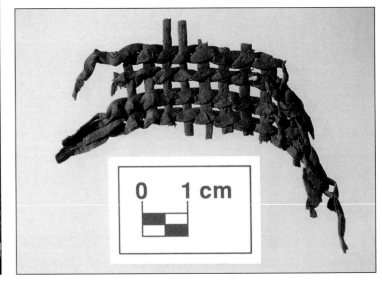

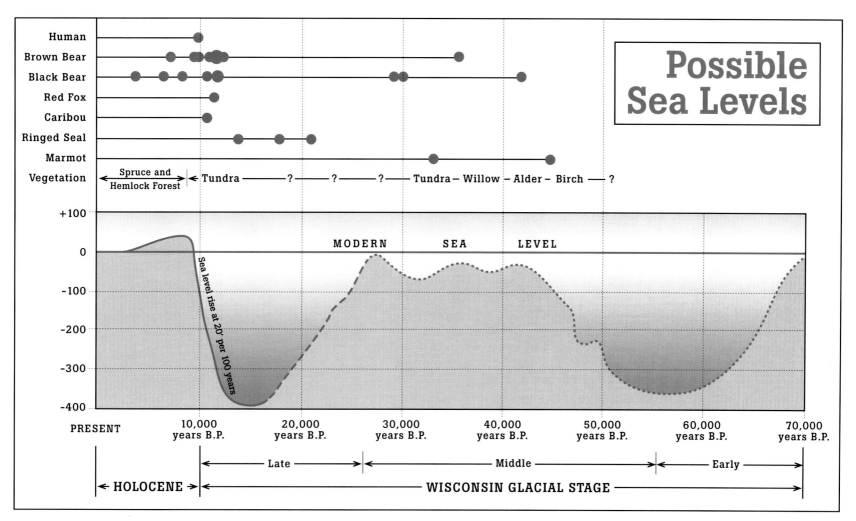

This graph shows possible sea levels throughout the Holocene and Wisconsin Glacial Stage for western Prince of Wales Island. The wavy line indicates estimated sea level trends. Sea levels prior to 16,000 years before present are speculative, with speculation increasing as the line moves to the right from dashes to dots. The upper portion of the figure shows the relative Carbon 14 dates of bones of mammals and possible associated vegetation recovered from caves on the island. (Source: Jim Baichtal, U.S. Forest Service)

Revillagigedo Island and Misty Fiords National Monument has not been researched. It is likely that many of the valleys of southern Southeast contained glaciers initiating from local ice caps and fields. There have been several glacial advances and retreats during the last 10,000 years, the last one beginning about 3,600 years ago and ending during the 18th and 19th centuries. Currently in southern Southeast only a few glaciers remain: Leduc, Chickamin, Soule, Through and Gracey Creek glaciers north and west of Hyder.

TOP: *A dark gray flint spear point, a notched piece of bone and a sea mammal rib used as a pressure-flaking tool to craft stone tools indicate the presence of early man among the islands of southern Southeast. (Terence Fifield, courtesy of U.S. Forest Service)*

ABOVE: *Two 1,300-year-old cedar boards, found beneath rock fall in an outer island cave, show evidence of traditional Northwest Coast design. Cedar cordage was found in place in the aligned holes in the board's edge. (Terence Fifield, courtesy of U.S. Forest Service)*

Putting People into the
Picture of the Changing Ecosystem.

Sometime before the end of the Pleistocene, before 12,500 years ago, people entered the North American scene. Scientists can be relatively certain of at least this statement. Archaeological discoveries at Monte Verde, Chile, dating to about 13,000 to 12,500 years ago as well as the firmly established Paleoindian traditions of the western United States support this idea. In fact, there are early man sites purported to be as old as 50,000 years in parts of the Americas. But most sites of those extreme ages are called into question for one reason or another.

In *Prehistoric Alaska* (1994) Dr. Bill Workman admirably described the archaeological thinking surrounding the first entry of humans into the Western Hemisphere. Workman reviews the variables involved in the model of this migration, the different environments that would have been encountered at different points in the prehistoric past, and the culture these immigrants might have brought with them. He also discusses the relatively new theory of a coastal migration route. The hypothesis of coastal migration, whether seen as a purposeful southward trek or a gradual expansion into new, and previously unoccupied territories, is particularly tantalizing to archaeologists working in Southeast.

The Bering Land Bridge concept and the vision of ice-age hunters expanding across the newly exposed tundralike plain has been the dominant theory of the peopling of the New World for many generations. That explanation remains a plausible one. But, in the last 20 years, archaeologists in British Columbia and Alaska have come increasingly to support the possibility that coastally adapted marine hunter/fisher/gatherers could have moved around the Pacific Rim from northern Asia into North America. Both before and after the last glacial maximum, at 22,000 to 17,000 years ago, ice conditions along the coast were such that there were no insurmountable impediments to the journey. With a lowering of worldwide sea level by as much as 390 feet about 17,000 years ago, the Northwest coast would have been a different place from what it is today. The emergent plain of the continental shelf would have been available in some areas as a travel corridor and hunting ground. Australian and Asian evidence indicates that boating technology was widespread as early as 40,000 years ago, and researchers can imagine these early North Americans as navigators, fishers and sea mammal hunters.

But, as Workman points out, the hard proof that people were on the Pacific Northwest coast before 10,000 years ago is entirely lacking. At present there are four archaeological sites in Southeast that predate 8,000 years ago, and several more in British Columbia.

Robert Ackerman's work at the Groundhog Bay site near Icy Strait in northern Southeast in the mid-1960s produced the first evidence of what has been called the Paleomarine tradition in Southeast Alaska. Component III at Groundhog Bay 2 contained biface fragments in the lowest level associated with a radio-carbon date of 9,200 years ago. In the same component was an assemblage of microblades between 8,900 and 4,150 years old.

At the Hidden Falls site on Baranof Island, Stan Davis reports a microblade assemblage in an ancient soil that is between 10,300 and 8,600 years old. The cultural materials themselves are thought to be no older than 9,500 years.

The multicomponent Chuck Lake site on Heceta Island has received the attention of several archaeological teams. Investigations were conducted in 1985 by Robert Ackerman of Washington State University; H. and A. Okada, a Japanese team from Hokkaido University in 1989 and 1991; and Wallace Olson, retired University of Alaska Southeast professor who accompanied the Okadas on both trips. Again, the oldest deposits at the site, located in Locality 1, contain microblades and micro-blade cores. The earliest dates at Chuck Lake are approximately 8,200 years before present.

On the southeast coast of Moresby Island in the Queen Charlotte Islands the *Gwaii Haanus* Archaeological Project is producing a wealth of information on past sea levels, environments and prehistoric human occupation. The single component site of Arrow Creek 2 is dated to approximately 9,200 years old, a date obtained from a radiocarbon date of a barnacle attached to a microblade.

Most recently, Tim Heaton, a paleontologist with the University of South Dakota, Vermillion, discovered a fragmentary human skeleton and tools in a cave on the north end of Prince of Wales Island. The cave, the site of paleontological investigations in 1994 and 1995, has returned a suite of radiocarbon dates on non-human skeletal remains ranging from more than 41,000 years ago to 1,900 years ago. Two radiocarbon dates on the human bones place their age at approximately 9,800 years. The tools, a lanceolate chert biface (spear point), a curved and

Test excavations in this dry rock shelter revealed cultural deposits, including the remains of mussels, clams, fish and land mammals, indications that people have camped in the shelter for 2,000 or more years. (Terence Fifield, courtesy of U.S. Forest Service)

FACING PAGE: *A commercial salmon seiner fishes open ocean waters off the southwestern shore of Dall Island. The 47-mile-long island has a convoluted coastline, the result of gouging and carving by prehistoric glaciers. (Craig J. Flatten)*

ABOVE: *This anthropomorphic petroglyph on an outer island is part of a grouping of 30 designs including concentric circles and masks. (Terence Fifield, courtesy of U.S. Forest Service)*

ABOVE RIGHT: *Stakes mark the excavation grid where scientists have found bear skeletons 7,000 to 12,000 years old. (Terence Fifield, courtesy of U.S. Forest Service)*

pointed bone tool, and a notched bone point fragment, offer enticing fuel for speculation.

There are few known archaeological sites on the Southeast coast that date to this early time. Explanations for the existence of these evidences of human presence have tended to focus on why there are so few sites, and why the sites are small with meager artifact assemblages. Scientists have speculated that hunter/gatherer groups may have moved to the coast for short periods of time, bringing tool technologies related to their interior origins. Finding life on the coast unacceptably rigorous, they may have abandoned their camps and returned inland.

However, some lines of evidence point toward other explanations. Obsidian, volcanic glass, from Suemez Island off the outer coast of Prince of Wales Island, is found as microblades in several of the sites noted above, as is obsidian from Mount Edziza in northcentral British Columbia. That this material is found in sites over a broad geographic range suggests a well-developed trade network or exchange system as long ago as 9,500 years. A second inference would be the existence of sophisticated watercraft and open-ocean navigation skills to obtain the Suemez obsidian and to account for its wide distribution.

As noted above, there is increasing evidence to support the notion that the outer islands and extensive portions of Prince of Wales Island were ice-free as early as 16,000 years ago. The discovery of comprehensive paleontological collections from the late Pleistocene provides clues to the changing environment; an environment that may have supported humans much earlier than presently known.

Why Don't Scientists Find Pleistocene Sites in Southeast?

If people were living on the coast before 10,000 years ago, even as early as 15,000 or 16,000 years ago, why don't researchers find the remains of their camps? Several reasons

A powerful rock art panel from Prince of Wales Island displays signs of recent vandalism. (Terence Fifield, courtesy of U.S. Forest Service)

come to mind. Generally, archaeologists imagine the first human occupants of the region to be a mobile group involved in a seasonal round of hunting, fishing and gathering. Such groups would have traveled light and made efficient use of resources, leaving scant evidence of their activities. Of perhaps greater impact is the passage of more than 10,000 years since those camps would have been used. The coastal rain forest of the Pacific Northwest has developed during those years. Trees have been uprooted many times by storms battering the coast. Conifers have dropped countless tons of dried foliage on the forest floor, creating a duff layer in many cases several feet thick. The acidic soils resulting from decay of conifer needles and twigs have hastened the deterioration of wood and bone objects dropped in the forest. In short, the archaeological evidence of these early sites may be extremely difficult to find and identify.

Perhaps the most significant factor affecting scientists' ability to find the camps of these late Pleistocene people is the changes in sea level that have accompanied the end of the Ice Age. As discussed earlier, several factors affect relative sea level change. The general implications for archaeology can be presented simply. If researchers assume late Pleistocene and early Holocene people concentrated their activities near the shore, as people did in historic and ethohistoric times, then most archaeological sites will be located near the shoreline as it was at the time of occupation. Generally, sea level reached its maximum on Prince of Wales Island about 10,000 years ago. Shoreline features of that age are found up to 20 feet above modern sea level. Archaeological sites of that time should be found at least the same distance above modern sea level and significantly back in the woods, and thus be hard to locate. Marine shell beds between 8,500 and 9,900 years old have been found exposed in stream cut banks 10 to 25 feet above modern low tide levels in more than 30 drainages on Prince of Wales. These fossil deposits would have been just below low tide levels at the time the clams lived. Graphing the elevation of these fossil clam beds against their ages allows a general projection of the rate and extent of sea level change during the last 10,000 years.

Before 10,000 years ago, sea level was rising relatively rapidly for a couple thousand years. Coastal campsites associated with hunters and fishers 12,000 or 13,000 years ago would today be deep under water. Carrying this idea to its extreme, a theoretical 17,000-year-old coastal camp would be up to 400 feet below modern sea level.

Current Research

Testing the hypothesis that humans were living on the coast of Southeast in the late Pleistocene hinges on finding archaeological evidence of that occupation. Several lines of research are being pursued. An intriguingly interrelated body of research is focused on describing the changing environment of Southeast through the end of the Ice Age and into more recent times. Glacial geologists, paleontologists, biologists and archaeologists are working with the common goal of understanding the environment at various points in its history, modeling change through time and identifying the first evidence of human presence on the land.

Geologic teams are scouring alpine areas on Prince of Wales and other islands for evidence of the extent and timing of past glacial advances and the direction of flow of ice masses. They are examining glacial till exposed in roadside excavations to determine sediment dynamics. Paleontological work on Pleistocene mammals is proceeding in the caves of Prince of Wales Island. The estuarine muds of the large streams in the region also hold promise because they are air-tight vaults of the organic remains of the past. Fossil pollen grains, plant parts, animal remains and even wood and bone artifacts may be preserved for thousands of years in these water-saturated muds now elevated above the deteriorating effects of salt water.

All these lines of study lead toward an understanding of the land and the ecosystem at a time when humans may have first entered the scene. If, in fact, people were living on the Southeast Alaska coast more than 10,000 years ago, understanding the setting and the changing location of sea level will vastly improve the chance of finding that evidence. ∎

This sentinel evergreen guards an islet in Klawock Lake, a good-sized lake inland from Klawock on Prince of Wales Island and drained by the Klawock River into Klawock Inlet. (Don Cornelius)

Ketchikan

By Patricia Roppel

EDITOR'S NOTE: *Patricia Roppel, Southeast Alaska resident for 36 years, has researched, traveled and photographed much of the region. She is the author of two issues of* ALASKA GEOGRAPHIC® *:* Southeast: Alaska's Panhandle *(1978) and* Sitka and Its Ocean/Island World *(1982). Her published books include* Alaska's Salmon Hatcheries, 1891-1959 *(1982),* Southeast Alaska: A Pictorial History *(1983),* Salmon From Kodiak *(1986),* Fortunes from the Earth *(1991), and An* Historical Guide to Revillagigedo and Gravina Islands *(1996). At present she lives in Wrangell.*

Clinging to steep hillsides along Tongass Narrows, Ketchikan is the first port of call for those who journey north from the "states" into Southeast Alaska. Commercial airlines and many vessels also make the city a farewell stop, the last impression of Alaska. No matter whether it is a first or a last stop, visitors see a linear city sprawled along the waterfront.

Ketchikan, perched on the rocky southwestern shore of Revillagigedo Island, is an isolated island city with no bridges to other islands or to the mainland. Here residents have always had to be ingenious to provide ways and means to be a largely self-sufficient community.

Original residents built the business district suspended on pilings above the sea. As time passed, the city's waterfront was gradually filled with rock and dredge material, thus expanding the narrow area between the mountains and deep water. As in the early days, many of its homes perch on rocky hillsides reached by wooden stairways or narrow, winding roads.

The waterfront pulses with constant activity and sounds: the deafening buzz of a departing floatplane, the quieter hum of boat engines, the rumble of tugs pulling gigantic barges piled high with cargo or aiding immense cruise ships to reach the docks. Overhead the scream of gulls remains a constant.

The same waters are a thoroughfare for fishing boats which have, since Ketchikan's earliest days, added to the town's role as a major Alaska fishing port. Today the seine, gillnet, troll and

FACING PAGE: *Stu Hoyt and Alan Henceroth survey Revillagigedo Island, Ketchikan, Tongass Narrows and Gravina Island with its airport from the summit of Deer Mountain. (Don Pitcher)*

An Alaska Marine Highway ferry waits at the terminal north of downtown Ketchikan. From Ketchikan ferries travel south along the Inside Passage to Bellingham, Wash., east along Portland Canal to Hyder, west to Hollis on Prince of Wales Island and south to Metlakatla on Annette Island. Northbound ferries call at several communities in the Panhandle. (Roy Corral)

crab boats share Tongass Narrows with floating processors and yachts. Skiffs ferry back and forth from a suburb community on Pennock Island. In nearby Clarence Strait and West Behm Canal, nuclear submarines head to a Navy noise testing facility on Back Island, north of town.

Another part of this maritime traffic is the blue–and–white Alaska Marine Highway System's ferries. This system started in 1963 to provide access between Southeast towns and Prince Rupert B.C. for passengers and cars, and later it expanded to Seattle. Now its southern terminus is Bellingham, Wash.

Every half an hour, the small ferry owned by the Ketchikan Gateway Borough takes passengers, cars and freight across Tongass Narrows to Ketchikan International Airport, which opened in 1973 on Gravina Island. Daily jet flights both north and south provide access to the island-bound community. Many dream that one day the two islands will be connected by a bridge, estimated to cost between $60 million and $130 million, thus eliminating the short ferry ride.

Long before white men reached the site of what is now known as Ketchikan, Tlingit Indians had a summer fishing camp on the banks of a creek where salmon returned in great numbers. The camp was known as *Kitschk-him* or Ketschk's stream, which is said to mean "spread wings of a prostrate eagle." Folklore ascribes this description to a midstream rock

Since Ketchikan is not connected to the continental highway system, boats and planes remain the only access. This view looking north up Tongass Narrows shows the airport on Gravina Island at upper left, Ketchikan Shipyard at right center, Bar Harbor for small boats at lower right and an Alaska Marine Highway ferry heading south at lower left. (Hall Anderson)

that divided the waters of the creek so as to suggest this image. Another account says the name came from the stream that ran full of pink salmon and thus was called *Kich-xaan* or Salmon Creek. These salmon attracted the first white men to the creek, where today visitors can still observe pink salmon ascending to spawn. In the winter of 1886-87 Tongass Packing Co. erected a cannery at Ketchikan, the white man's pronunciation and spelling of the Indian name. During the summers of the next two years, fishermen hauled seines full of salmon from the creek, Chinese workers butchered and packed the fish into cans that they had made by hand before the runs started. Then in mid-1889, the cannery buildings were consumed by fire and the site was abandoned.

With a stream where fish swarmed body to body upstream, it can be expected other entrepreneurs would follow. Mike Martin, often considered the City Father, and his partner George Clark built a salmon saltery and trading post around 1890, but within eight years their enterprise failed.

What revived the town was gold. Prospectors found this glittering metal in paying quantities in nearby hills, on the mainland and on Prince of Wales Island. Then commercial quantities of copper were discovered, and Ketchikan became an important rendezvous point for miners, prospectors and businessmen.

By the time Ketchikan was incorporated on Aug. 25, 1900,

ABOVE LEFT: *Log bundles are readied for transfer to a ship. The timber industry in southern Southeast has generated heated debate in recent years that culminated in an agreement in early 1997 between the federal government and a private company to make available a three-year supply of timber from Tongass National Forest for sawmills in Ketchikan and on Annette Island. (Don Cornelius)*

LEFT: *A mainstay of Ketchikan's economy for many years, the Louisiana Pacific pulp mill at Ward Cove, northwest of downtown Ketchikan, closed in March 1997. (Roy Corral)*

Ferry passengers cruise past the Whipple Creek clear-cut in Tongass Narrows. (Don Cornelius)

it was a booming mining center with a population of 800. Carpenters, saloon keepers, clerks, store owners, attorneys, doctors arrived. Churches, a school, new business buildings and multistoried and turreted homes sprung up: a microcosm of today's town. A transportation company ran boats, today replaced by air taxis, to the outlying camps. Mining continued to be a major industry until 1907 when the copper market collapsed and local mines closed permanently. The mining industry during the next 90 years waxed and mostly waned, and today mining is not significant to the economy of Ketchikan. However, prospecting continues and old mines are being explored with modern technology. A molybdenum mine at Quartz Hill, on the mainland south of town, is on hold until prices rise for the mineral. Plans to reopen some of the old marble quarries at Calder and on Tuxekan and Marble islands are coming to a head in 1997. Ketchikan entrepreneurs look forward to the time when these operations will again stimulate the local economy.

It was the fishing industry that grew in importance after that first crash in mining in 1907. Ketchikan began its climb toward "salmon capital of the world" status. Fidalgo Island Packing Co., which put up its first canned salmon pack in 1900, was the only cannery until 1912 when three new ones began to operate. Through the years, new salmon canneries were built until, in 1936, seven local plants produced more than 1.5 million cases, a figure that does not include the pack of one of the larger operations. This is more than 36 million individual cans!

With the addition in 1908 of New England Fish Co.'s cold storage plant, and five years later, Ketchikan Cold Storage, the waterfront was dominated by fish-processing plants. Related support businesses, such as machine shops and ship's chandleries, sprung up as well. For those who drive and walk along the waterfront today, many of these same buildings, transformed by different uses, can still be seen. Historic Ketchikan Inc. is working on documenting these buildings, and it is hoped the organization will erect signage to inform locals and visitors alike of the buildings' historical contributions, as it has done along the historical district of Stedman and Thomas streets.

Ketchikan remains an active fishing center and headquarters for a large fleet, but today, with the change in emphasis on fish processing, only four canneries continue to pack salmon, some on a limited basis. Ward Cove Packing Co. has the distinction of having canned salmon every season since its founding in 1912, except in 1971 when no fish were packed locally. Trident Fisheries, at the original Fidalgo Island Co.'s plant, continues to put salmon in the can with updated machinery and processes that would have astonished the original 1900 crews. Farther south along the waterfront, Alaska General Processors operates a small cannery mainly for salmon. Silver Lining/Norquest Seafoods also cans both fresh and smoked salmon in a building that since 1920 has housed numerous other canning operations.

Canning salmon is not the only method for preserving fish.

Although downtown Ketchikan doesn't receive a lot of snow, the mountains of Revillagigedo Island behind the town stop the abundant moisture sweeping in off the Pacific Ocean and experience snowfall in winter. (Hall Anderson)

Fresh king salmon were first commercially shipped out on ice in 1903. Now trollers commercially fish for kings during a short June season. Several local shippers and many of the cold storage plants ship out fresh whole fish and fillets of various species of salmon and halibut. Some travel by refrigerated vanloads on the ferries and others aboard airplanes.

Freezing is another processing method. Fishing vessels unload halibut and salmon at the old New England Fish Co. cold storage dock that is now owned and operated by Trident Fisheries. E. C. Phillips and Son, Silver Lining/Norquest Seafoods and Alaska General Processors also ship frozen fish to market in freezer vans on the ferries.

Diversification in the fishing industry is the byword today because commercial salmon fishing is highly seasonal. Fishermen and processor crews generally are employed two to four months per year unless they work in multiple fisheries. Processing different species of seafood makes it possible for a company to run year-round. Herring (both bait and food), Dungeness crab, black cod (sometimes called sablefish) and shrimp or prawns have been part of the economy for several decades. Markets have been developed and divers and crews trained to harvest and process geoducks and sea cucumbers. In 1996, after test fisheries financed by the seafood industry and local governments, a viable red sea urchin fishery has started production. Sea cucumbers and urchin eggs are prized in Japan.

Fishing, as a basic economy, has shared the stage with harvest of another renewable resource — timber. In the heart of downtown Ketchikan, Alaska's oldest continuously operated manufacturing industry, Ketchikan Spruce Mills, operated from 1903 to 1983. At first it cut lumber for the fast-growing communities of Southeast, then adapted to the needs of the Panhandle's booming economy by producing shook for canned salmon boxes, ties for the construction of the Alaska Railroad, Sitka spruce for aircraft construction during World War II, piano sounding boards and string instruments. Cants or squared sections of log became an important export during the 1970s and 1980s. These were generally sent to Japan for remanufacture of traditional products. More recently the demand for cants has diminished.

Demand for pulp wood fueled the timber industry's interest and fired Ketchikan's economy. North of town, across the cove from Ward Cove Packing Co., is Ketchikan Pulp Co. operated by Louisiana Pacific Corp. since 1977. This multimillion-dollar plant was completed in 1954, culminating efforts by the federal and territorial governments that had begun in the 1920s to encourage the pulp industry in Alaska.

The city's infrastructure had to be upgraded and facilities readied for the thousand-plus workers and their families who came to run the mill and provide logs. Much of the housing built above Newtown, the hospital, new schools and the University of Alaska's community college were the result of the arrival of this new industry. Water Street, at that time the sole corridor between downtown Ketchikan and Saxman and everything to the north, was a plank street on pilings, skirting the rock ridge that separates the old from the newer parts of town. A tunnel was blasted through the ridge; the rubble used for fill, and it became what the *Guinness Book of World Records* calls the only tunnel in the world one can drive through, around and over.

To accommodate the increased traffic, highways to the south and the north were widened, lengthened and paved so that today Tongass Highway totals 31 miles. With the miles of streets within the city limits, the system provides 53 miles of road. A driver on the North Tongass Highway goes past McDonald's, the indoor mall, the ferry dock, the post office, the airport ferry dock, the Ward Cove cannery, the pulp mill and

ends at Settler's Cove campground. South Tongass Highway runs through the Native community of Saxman, several housing developments, the suburbs of Mountain Point and Herring Cove, the Whitman Lake hatchery, and ends at George Inlet Cannery, where today Cape Fox Native Corp. provides a tour of the building and displays to acquaint people with Ketchikan's fishing past.

For nearly 40 years, giant log rafts could be seen being towed along the narrow waterways from one of the many logging camps in the vicinity to the pulp mill at Ward Cove. By 1996, Ketchikan's long-standing timber industry was in jeopardy because of the national movement away from timber harvest on federal lands, especially old-growth timber. Surrounded by Tongass National Forest, Ketchikan's source of logs was reduced significantly. Because of this, Ketchikan Pulp Mill announced it would close the Ward Cove plant in March 1997. The mill accounted for 6 to 7 percent of local jobs, and its closure cost the economy many more jobs in support industries and services and in businesses that rely on workers' spending.

When it is too steep for vehicles, streets in Ketchikan turn into stairways. Here is the intersection of Jackson Street and Third Avenue. (Judith Erickson)

After months of uncertainty, negotiations between the federal government and Louisiana Pacific resulted in the announcement in late February 1997 that an agreement had been reached for a three-year supply of timber to keep KPC's sawmills operating. This will support about 400 KPC sawmill workers, loggers and related timber workers. The Ketchikan Sawmill, next door to the pulp mill, and Annette Hemlock Mill in Metlakatla will continue operating. What will become of the pulp facility and/or the site is under discussion, and the city and borough governments have already begun to study future uses.

Today, Ketchikan is leaning heavily on expansion of its tourism industry. Visitors are nothing new: Tourists started coming to Alaska more than a century ago. Today nearly half the visitors touring Alaska are introduced to the state in Ketchikan. Luxury passenger ships, often immaculately white, tie up at the downtown waterfront or anchor in the Narrows from April through September. In 1996 these ships made 494 stops, bringing 426,350 people. Including those who come by ferry and air, approximately a half million people visited in 1996. The number of visitors is expected to increase in 1997.

What entices visitors to Ketchikan? One is its Native culture. Before the white man, Tlingits relied on the forest to build many

ABOVE LEFT: *While a rain cloud bumps up against the mountains behind Ketchikan, a shaft of afternoon sun highlights the town's famous welcome sign. Ketchikan is the first major port of call for ships heading north up the Inside Passage from the Pacific Northwest. The sign spans Mission Street, flanked by the Ingersoll Hotel on the left and some of the many downtown gift shops on the right. (Penny Rennick)*

LEFT: *Cruise ships, sometimes several at a time, dock adjacent to Front Street. Passengers can walk down the gangplank to find the Ketchikan Visitor Information Center, tour buses, horse-drawn tour coaches, and, just across the street, a several block area of visitor attractions, gift shops, and dining and lodging establishments. (Penny Rennick)*

The Totem Heritage Center, a short walk uphill from downtown, displays several authentic 19th-century totem poles. The exhibits, both indoors and outdoors, give a good overview of Northwest Coast Native cultures, and the walk to the center follows Ketchikan Creek, offering a glimpse into residential Ketchikan, its stairway streets, narrow pathways and lush gardens. (Don Pitcher)

essentials of their lifestyle. Canoes and homes of cedar or spruce were hand hewn. Cedar totem poles in front of the houses kept alive the memory of important events and legends.

Today collections of this sophisticated art form are found in two parks and at the Totem Heritage Center. At Totem Bight State Historical Park, 10 miles north of downtown, a short trail winds through remnants of the rain forest, emerging into a saltwater setting where a replica of a community house and 15 totem poles stand. This project, as well as the one at Saxman, were developed by the U. S. Forest Service Civilian Conservation Corps in the late 1930s. At Saxman, 2.3 miles south from downtown along the Tongass Highway, local Natives have built a replica of a community house near the totems. Here flamboyant Tlingit dancers perform their intricate dances to introduce visitors to their culture.

The Totem Heritage Center, located along Ketchikan Creek, displays Alaska's only group of original totem poles. These were salvaged in the late 1960s from former Tlingit and Haida village sites in southern Southeast. In addition, a collection of contemporary Northwest Coast Indian art crafted during Native cultural classes can be seen. Displays describe trade beads used by early fur traders, Native regalia and fish camp life similar to what took place at the mouth of Ketchikan Creek prior to building of the first cannery.

Visitors and locals stop at the city's museum where Native and Russian cultures, nautical and fishing history, and western living tell more about how it was to live in this remote town in earlier times.

Ketchikan also remembers and capitalizes on another

aspect of its heritage, Creek Street, the famous red-light district where Dolly, Black Mary, Blind Polly, Frenchie, Nell and others plied their trade for more than half a century until 1954. About 20 houses once lined the hillside or were built on piles over Ketchikan Creek. Not many original structures remain, but new buildings have gone up to replace ramshackled and burned-out structures along the boardwalk. These newer buildings house shops and businesses. No. 24 Creek Street was the home and house of "sporting woman" Dolly Arthur for more than 50 years. Now it is a museum where Dolly's dishes, furniture, clothes, needlework and cash box are on display in a setting that remains essentially as it was in 1920 during Prohibition.

Misty Fiords National Monument is one of Ketchikan's chief visitor attractions: a spectacular scenic wilderness that can be reached only by boat or airplane. The people of Ketchikan have long visited, explored and admired the network of waterways and sheer polished cliffs carved and molded by massive glaciers more than 10,000 years ago. Now most people visit under the guidance of charter boat operators and air taxi tours. Boat travelers, after a 50-mile run from Ketchikan, slowly cruise the silent waters of the coves and view the old-growth forest. After about a 20-minute ride for those who choose to come by airplane, the visitors view spectacular hanging valleys, moraines, gull rookeries and glacier-carved cirques with their bowl-shaped lakes. Kayakers and canoeists glide silently and camp on deserted shores. Yachts anchor in protected bays while eagles soar overhead and curious harbor seals poke their heads out of the still water. Several U.S. Forest Service trails are available for use by the hardy.

BELOW LEFT: *Interactive exhibits on the flora and fauna, Native cultures and early history of southern Southeast, and a trip-planning library and knowledgeable staff await visitors to the Southeast Alaska Visitor Center, a short, level walk from the visitor complex by the cruise ship dock. (Penny Rennick)*

BELOW: *There's nothing subtle about the living room of Dolly's House, now a museum but formerly the home of Dolly Arthur, one of Creek Street's "ladies of the line." (Alaska Division of Tourism)*

The Native community of southern Southeast actively participates in Ketchikan events. This contingent of Tlingits joins the July 4th parade through the city center in 1966. (Steve McCutcheon)

For many visitors and locals alike the irresistible lure is the king salmon, ranging from 10 to 60 pounds. Sportfishing is a fast-growing element in the local economy. There are several parts to this industry: charter boats, fishing lodges and local sportfisheries. One of the favorite sportfishing outings is the annual Ketchikan King Salmon Derby, where men, women and children troll for the largest salmon.

Visitors try their luck during king season from local resorts and nearby lodges. Passengers fly by floatplane to Prince of Wales Island to such places as Coffman Cove Wilderness Lodge, the Gold Coast Lodge in Moira Sound, Sportsman's Cove Lodge at Saltery Cove, Clover Bay Lodge and Waterfall Resort. Closer to Ketchikan, Yes Bay Lodge and Silver King Lodge can be reached by a short hop in a plane or boat. Visitors and fishermen also find accommodations and fishing at Clover Pass Resort and Salmon Falls Resort, both north of town and accessible by road. At Salmon Falls Resort, check out the outstanding collection of Native arts and crafts.

When salmon runs were at a low in the early 1950s, the Ketchikan Chamber of Commerce in 1954 raised money to build the Deer Mountain hatchery in the charming little City Park that had earlier been landscaped around the rearing ponds from a 1920s territorial hatchery. Various agencies have operated the Deer Mountain hatchery throughout the years. During the 1950s and 1960s, the hatchery reared mostly coho salmon. Later it branched out to include king salmon and steelhead trout. In 1985, returns were so great the hatchery was able to take all the necessary eggs and then open Ketchikan Creek for its first subsistence fishery, a practice that continues today.

Now Ketchikan Tribal Hatchery, a subsidiary of Ketchikan Indian Corp., owns and operates the facility. About 350,000 king and coho salmon and steelhead smolts are raised and released annually. A guided tour describes the salmon's life cycle and people can watch hatchery operations taking place in season.

Whitman Lake hatchery, operated by Southern Southeast Regional Aquaculture Association, south of town at Herring Cove, also produces salmon. A central incubation facility, Whitman Lake hatchery raises fry for release at various locations

BELOW LEFT: *The spectacular geology and scenery of Misty Fiords National Monument is one of the top draws for Ketchikan visitors. Cruise operators headquartered in Ketchikan offer excursions to the monument, and large cruise ships plying the Inside Passage also navigate the fiordlike waters of Rudyerd Bay's Punchbowl Cove. (Steve McCutcheon)*

BELOW: *Fishing, both commercial and sport, is one of the keystones of Ketchikan's economy. Anyone with a hook, line and pole, and the appropriate license if necessary, can try their hand at the mouth of Ketchikan Creek where it flows into Thomas Basin. These youngsters are bringing home a salmon for their afternoon's efforts. (Penny Rennick)*

ABOVE: *J. Darald DeWitt is one of several Native carvers who sharpen their skills at the carving center at Saxman, two miles south of Ketchikan. Tlingit Indians established the village in 1894, when Tongass and Cape Fox Natives combined their villages at a site chosen for a school. The community is named for Samuel Saxman, a teacher who arrived in southern Southeast Dec. 1, 1886, and drowned later that month while helping the Tlingits find a school site. (Don Pitcher)*

ABOVE RIGHT: *Ten miles out the North Tongass Highway north of Ketchikan is Totem Bight State Park with a clan house and several totems. (Harry M. Walker)*

throughout southern Southeast. These coho and king smolts and chum fry are reared and released at such locations as Shrimp Bay, Naket Bay, Earl West Cove, Kendrick Bay, and the returning adults are fished by the commercial fleet. The association also operates a larger hatchery at Neets Bay, which indents Revillagigedo Island in Behm Canal. Many sportsmen enjoy the increased fishing provided by the returning coho and king salmon en route to this hatchery.

Tourism is expected to become even bigger. The waterfront now has a dock that can handle 800-foot vessels. The Cape Fox tram moves people up the hillside to the Westmark Cape Fox

Lodge and the Ted Ferry Civic Center, a multipurpose public facility, which hosts conventions as well as local events. Downtown on the site of the original sawmill, the U. S. Forest Service built a $7-million interpretive center, the Southeast Alaska Visitor Center, to acquaint visitors with what they will see in the area. The exhibit rooms feature inform-ational displays on the rain forest, Native traditions, ecosystems and resources. Many find the trip-plan room a great help.

Several buildings to house curio shops, the new restaurant Steamers, and offices were constructed and opened in 1996 and early 1997 also on the former spruce mill site. Further development is planned including a marina and a large hotel that will have waterfront views.

For those who live here year-round, the town has much to offer. Approximately 8,500 people reside in the city and when those who live in the Ketchikan Gateway Borough are added, the population is around 14,000, making it the state's

ABOVE: *Just south of downtown, the U.S. Coast Guard maintains a base along Tongass Narrows. Among the top 10 employers in terms of number of jobs in Ketchikan, the Coast Guard has an annual average employment of more than 200. (Harry M. Walker)*

ABOVE RIGHT: *A submarine from the Navy's test facility near Back Island plies the waters of West Behm Canal. (Craig J. Flatten)*

fourth-largest city, behind Anchorage, Fairbanks and Juneau.

The population of the town is diverse. A great many of the current residents or their ancestors arrived from various parts of the "states." In addition, fishing helped attract a wide ethnic mix. Norwegians dominated the halibut industry. Japanese, Chinese and Filipino workers came by the hundreds to work in the canneries. Some stayed and started businesses, especially restaurants. Of the original inhabitants, the 1990 census enumerates the Haida, Tsimshian, Tlingit and other Natives at 15.7 percent of the population.

Those who live here permanently enjoy good public and private schools, as well as the college that is part of the University of Alaska Southeast. There is a fine city library as well as one at the university. Banks, numerous shops, food markets and a covered mall with several businesses provide basic needs as well as specialty items. An excellent hospital, family and specialist doctors, outreach programs, the Pioneers' Home and long-term care for the elderly are but a few of the medical services available. As in any large town, state and federal government services are numerous. For those who don't keep their boats beside their houses, there is moorage in five small boat harbors near easily accessible marine fueling docks. Art and humanities programs include out-of-town guest performers and the ever-popular Monthly Grind, a potpourri of local music, photography, drama and writing.

Although tourists may comment on the rain, especially if they have experienced the cause of one of the town's nicknames, "The Rain Capital of Alaska," most locals don't seem to mind the average of 154 inches of rain. That is nearly 13 feet of precipitation that drenches the city every year. The year's accumulated downpour is measured on a large rain gauge located near the Ketchikan Visitor's Bureau.

Those locals who thrive on outdoor activities enjoy the infrequent snow that brings out the cross-country skiers, snow-shoers, snowmobilers, four-wheelers and sledders to enjoy winter recreation. Ice skaters and hockey players rush to Ward Lake and then hope the temperatures stay below freezing for a while.

Winter festivals at Harriet Hunt Lake find families, children and dogs enjoying the revelry. Another celebration is the annual Blueberry Festival that includes a race where children encourage their slugs to slither first from the center to the outside of a ring. In the annual rubber duck race each July 4th, yellow rubber ducks are tossed into Ketchikan Creek and the first to survive the hazards of rushing water and to cross the finish line wins.

Spring, summer and fall find hikers on the trails that lead through the rain forest of hemlock, spruce, cedar, pine and alder. A favorite is the switchback path to the 3,000-foot summit and alpine meadows of Deer Mountain where there are fabulous views of Ketchikan and nearby islands. Another is the forest service boardwalk trail that climbs through the dark, mossy forest to Perseverance Lake, formed in a glacial cirque. The loop

BELOW LEFT: *The elegant Westmark Cape Fox Lodge sits astride a bluff overlooking downtown. Vehicle passengers can reach the lodge by driving up the back side of the bluff, but most visitors take the enclosed, Swedish-made funicular that begins on Creek Street and rises 100 feet to the lodge. (Penny Rennick)*

BELOW: *Numerous small businesses catering to visitors and outdoor recreationists have found a home in Ketchikan. Geoff Gross built his business, Southeast Exposure, around the many waterways of southern Southeast. (Don Pitcher)*

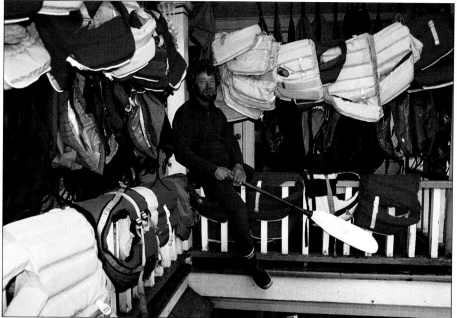

Businesses flank Water Street in an area of town that Ketchikan residents call New Town. Water Street leads north to a shopping mall, the hospital, the ferry terminal and many of the newer business complexes. New Town is separated from downtown by a tunnel at the north end of Front Street. The tunnel, completed in 1954, channels northbound traffic. Southbound vehicles drive around the outside of the tunnel, and traffic headed for residences on Nob Hill can drive over the tunnel. (Harry M. Walker)

path around Ward Lake draws many who don't want an extended hike.

When sunny days arrive, picnickers and swimmers can be found at Ward Lake, Settler's Cove (one of the area's few sandy beaches) and Refuge Cove State Recreational Site with its panoramic view of the Danger Islands. Bugge Beach, developed by the local Rotary Club, is also a favorite swimming hole made by a dam that captures sea water after high tides.

Organized sports attract many. Schools have competitive

The Baranof Queen, *a portion of its deck covered with salmon, plies the waters of George Inlet. Southeast and Canadian fishermen have been at odds over who can fish which salmon. Canadians say Southeast fishermen are taking more than their share of salmon, thus adding to the depletion of salmon stocks that spawn in British Columbia rivers. (Hall Anderson)*

swimming, volleyball, basketball and wrestling teams. Baseball and football leagues attract the younger set. Softball brings out adult teams. Runners participate in numerous races sponsored throughout the year. For others who aren't into competition, there is a new bike trail from town to Saxman, swimming at two indoor pools and several health clubs. The opportunities are endless.

And opportunity is a word frequently heard in town these days. Ketchikan has survived and grown and generally prospered with its diverse economy. As one resource neared exhaustion or its market weakened, city planners have sought and so far found another. With the disclosure that Ketchikan Pulp Co., the area's largest employer, would close, the Borough Assembly announced plans to invest in the state's Ketchikan Shipyard to make the operation economical and provide jobs, to put out a request for a specialist to market the Ward Cove mill site, to contribute to further development of the sea urchin fishery, and to push for development of an industrial park near Lewis Reef. Several businesses have sent letters of interest in this Gravina Island site including ventures involving fishing gear storage, fish and wood by-products composting, an emergency oil response center, a sawmill and fish-freight business.

In addition to the Borough, others in the community are promoting Mahoney Lake power, an aquarium, housing for university students, construction of a value-added wood processing plant, and a better ferry system between Metlakatla, Prince of Wales Island and Ketchikan.

Today's First City residents and planners have accepted the challenge to assure the continued economic health of and the livability for everyone in the community. ▮

Echoes of an Alaska Boomtown: Loring, 1870 to 1930

By Jeanne T. Gerulskis

EDITOR'S NOTE: *As senior curator of programs for Ketchikan Museums, Jeanne curated an exhibition on Loring's history for Tongass Historical Museum in 1996. This article is drawn from her exhibition text, for which fellow staff members Brenda Abney, Karla Sunderland, Risa Carlson, Ann Thomson and Richard Van Cleave helped gather much of the information. Originally a Bostonian, Jeanne hitchhiked to Seward with her friend Deb Cole in 1978, and then followed an Alaska-style career path of fish cleaner, bartender, log scaler, musician and ferry terminal assistant before deciding to enter the museum field in 1989.*

In the years when Ketchikan was just getting its start, the village of Loring was an exciting, growing community, with businesses, a post office and the world's largest cannery and hatchery. Today, while approximately 14,700 people live within the boundaries of Ketchikan Gateway Borough and almost half a million summer visitors make Ketchikan their first port of call, only a handful of people own homes in the quiet, remote village site of Loring, and only one or two people make it their year-round residence.

Saltery

For centuries, Natives had come to the Naha River area for the same reason that led to the founding of Loring. The beautiful wilderness that encompasses the Naha River teems with eagles, bears, deer — and salmon. Lots of salmon. Somehow, a group of investors in San Francisco got wind of the tales of the Naha, with its unbelievably rich stock of salmon. In 1882, they asked the U.S. Coast and Geodetic Survey to help locate a site where large vessels could dock in the Naha area. In response, the U.S. Navy charted Naha Bay. On April 20, 1883, the Alaska Salmon Packing and Fur Co. incorporated in San Francisco; later that year, the company built a saltery on Naha Bay near the area's impressive waterfalls.

FACING PAGE: *Loring photographer, shopkeeper, postmaster and entrepreneur Con Giebel (second from right) poses with Captain Rasmussen (far right) and company on the* Star of Scotland, *the Alaska Packers Association ship that first brought Giebel to Loring in 1908. (Photo by Cornelius E. Giebel, Tongass Historical Society Collection #73.3.16.237)*

Heckman Lake, near Loring, was reportedly named for J. R. Heckman, superintendent of the Loring cannery and inventor of the Heckman Floating Fish Trap. (Don Pitcher)

In the late 1800s, while salting was a standard way to preserve fish, operating a saltery was still an exciting new venture in Southeast. During the height of the season, Loring bustled with activity, as salmon caught in nets in the lake and in the bay by the falls were washed, split and boned by Native men and women, and then salted, barreled and loaded onto ships. Other fish-related enterprises flourished in turn-of-the-century Loring, including two companies that made lubricating and medicinal oils from the livers of dogfish — sharks that fed off the salmon refuse discarded by the Loring fish processors.

The site where the saltery was located had been known as Naha Bay, possibly based on a Tlingit term for "the country of distant lakes." When Alaska Salmon Packing and Fur Co. investor Max Pracht moved to Alaska in 1885 as superintendent of the saltery, he renamed the area Loring. Whoever Loring was — an Indian agent, a company investor, a personal friend — his or her identity has been obliterated by time. But the community was officially established as Loring when Assistant Saltery Superintendent, Storekeeper and Postmaster Emilio N. Terello opened Alaska's most southerly post office on Sept. 20, 1885.

Despite its remote location, Loring at the turn of the century had a surprising number of modern amenities. It was the first stop for steamers from the West Coast, and the central distribution point for mail for other settlements, canneries and mission stations for miles around. The community was also linked to the outside world via telephone. The phone line reached from the Loring cannery, around the head of Naha Bay, and through miles of cedar, spruce and hemlock to Ketchikan until 1907, when the telephone line was relaid along the beach. Loring's, and later Ketchikan's, famous resident J.R. Heckman opened a general store for Loring residents and visitors in 1885, with his brother, H.E. Heckman, in charge. The H.E. Heckman and Co. store was a major feature of Loring's landscape for decades, as the J.R. Heckman block remains a feature of Ketchikan today.

Cannery

As things were going well with the saltery, the Alaska Salmon Packing and Fur Co. made a decision that would shape

Loring into a major player in the fledgling Alaska seafood industry. The company decided to build a cannery, to be operated by the Cutting Packing Co., at the mouth of Naha Bay. Completed in 1888, the Loring cannery produced 18,771 cases of salmon in its first season. While the saltery continued to operate for several more years, it was rapidly outshone by the cannery, and eventually closed.

More and more ships started docking at Loring to bring in mail, supplies, work crews and even tourists, and to load up on canned and salted salmon to deliver to West Coast ports.

A year after the Loring cannery began production, there were 37 canneries in operation in Alaska. This proved more than the market could bear; within three years, more than half of these new canneries closed. To improve their economic position, the Alaska Packing and Fur Co. joined first with a number of other canneries under a temporary organization called the Alaska Salmon Canners in 1891, and then in 1892 with an organization known as the Alaska Packing Association, in which the Alaska Packing and Fur Co. was issued stock. In 1893, the Alaska Packing Association reorganized into the Alaska Packers Association (APA), incorporating 22 companies into a powerful entity. The old Alaska Packing and Fur Co. became part of APA, which issued the Alaska Packing and Fur Co. stock in exchange for its Loring cannery.

In its first year, with nine canneries in operation, APA accounted for 70 percent of the total Alaska salmon pack. In the next six years, it approached monopoly status on the supply of Alaska canned salmon, with an annual average of 80.2 percent of the pack. APA continued expanding the number of canneries it operated, and began building a fleet of vessels — steam launches, steamers, barkentines and iron-hulled ships including its famed "Star" ships. The Loring operation fared so well that APA began building a new, considerably larger cannery in Loring on the site of the old cannery in 1901. People who worked for APA in Loring by providing fish or as cannery hands included Tsimshian and Tlingit who made their homes in Loring, Port Chester, Cape Fox and other nearby villages; white men and women who traveled from the West Coast to work each season; and the China crew.

China Crew

The season began each April with the arrival from San Francisco of APA's first supply vessel. On board were laborers, fishermen, gear and supplies, including tin plate for making cans, pig lead, soldering crystals, caustic soda, lacquer, oil, coal, labels and food for the Chinese and white crews. Unloading the ship was the first task. Then came the labor-intensive jobs of making the cans, preparing the nets and other gear, getting the fishing boats shipshape, setting up the kitchens and supply areas, and doing all the preparations that would ensure a smooth operation once the fish run started. Cutting the sheets of tin plate to the proper size and soldering each can together to produce enough cans to handle the enormous Loring pack was quite a job. It took the Chinese crew the entire period from their arrival in April to the mid- to late-June fish run to complete this task.

To ensure an affordable, reliable labor force for its canneries, the canning industry engaged in "China contracts." A Chinese-owned company based in San Francisco, Seattle or another West Coast city would negotiate the China contract with cannery management. The Chinese company generally included in its price the labor costs of a crew to work in the cannery, a cook, all food needed for the season, a "China boss" (crew foreman) and some profit for the Chinese company. The cannery company guaranteed a minimum number of cases packed for the season, and paid the Chinese company a fixed amount per case. If the pack exceeded the minimum guarantee, the Chinese company would be paid a certain amount per extra case packed; if the pack was less than anticipated, the Chinese company still got paid its guaranteed amount. Out of this amount, the Chinese company directly paid the Chinese cannery workers their wages. The China crew had their own housing and their own mess hall in Loring, where traditional Chinese food was prepared by their own cook. To handle the huge volume of salmon and to ensure profits for both the cannery and the Chinese company, the Chinese crew was required to work almost around the clock during the height of the salmon season.

The men who came to Loring via the China contract listed their nationality and place of birth as China, but their home as San Francisco. The majority listed their San Francisco occupations as laborers. But some of Loring's Chinese workers earned a living as laundry men, farmers, farmhands, shoemakers, cooks, merchants, cigar makers, shirtmakers, bookkeepers and porters during the winter season.

The China contract workers were all men, and all citizens of China. To escape a life of poverty in China for themselves and their families, Chinese men came to America to work. But state and federal legislation prohibited them from becoming Americans. Their wives could not accompany them to the United States. And if they returned to China to see their families, they could not gain re-entry into the United States. In some states, they could not marry non-Chinese women; in other states, they could marry non-Chinese women only at the loss of U.S. citizenship for their wives.

Season after season, Chinese workers returned to Loring and played a critical role in the salmon canning operation, then returned south. Hundreds of Chinese men dwelt amid the cedar and spruce trees, the rivers and waterfalls. Today, broken pieces of ginger jars and other Chinese pottery scattered through the forest, and photographs and company records housed in libraries and museum archives, bear witness to their lives and labors.

By 1904, Japanese were also working at the Loring cannery. The contract began to be known as the "Oriental contract," and soon Mexicans, Italians, Filipinos, Puerto Ricans and

Built in 1901, the new Alaska Packers Association cannery at Loring supported a large population of workers until 1930 when the great fishing boom died down and the cannery was dismantled. (Tongass Historical Museum Collection #74.6.10.17a)

Chinese all worked on the Loring crew, each nationality with their own housing and mess halls.

J.R. Heckman and the Floating Fish Trap

James Robert Heckman, Nova Scotia-born and California-raised, began his association with Loring by working at the Loring cannery as a machinist's helper. At age 24, J.R. Heckman became foreman of the Loring cannery. When the cannery came under the ownership of APA, Heckman became its superintendent, a position he was to hold for a quarter century. In 1895, he constructed his first floating fish trap.

Native people had used fish weirs constructed of spruce roots and fish traps made of rocks for millennia. They were an efficient means of catching fish for subsistence, but did not deplete the resource. The Loring cannery, as a large-scale commercial operation, needed many more fish than would be obtainable by using traditional weirs and traps. Consequently, the cannery at Loring used commercial fish traps, both stationary and floating.

Early commercial fish traps were either hand set or stationary. J.R. Heckman's floating trap was less expensive to build and maintain. The stationary traps required large piles obtainable only in Canada and Washington state. Government regulations required that driven piles be removed at the end of each season, which often resulted in piles breaking during removal. Storing floating traps for the winter was much easier because they could be towed to a sheltered spot. Federal legislation prohibiting the placement of traps in streams and estuaries also encouraged the use of floating traps. Heckman patented his design in 1908, and sold numerous rights for this design at $500 each, quite a hefty sum in those days. Floating fish traps proliferated in Southeast.

The era of fish traps was an exciting time. Traps were loaded with salmon, and trap guards fought with fish pirates — or were occasionally bribed to look the other way. After World War I, trap robbers began arming themselves, and shooting to kill. Federal and territorial agencies organized patrols to prevent fish piracy. Trap guards carried rifles. Canneries employed

Canned and salted salmon carrying labels by the Alaska Packers Association cannery at Loring made their way to ports up and down the West Coast. This label from 1906 describes its simple recipe as just one pound of fresh salmon and one-quarter ounce of salt cooked in the sealed can. (Tongass Historical Museum)

private detectives. But fish pirates were rarely caught, and if caught, were often acquitted or given light sentences.

Fish traps had done their job too well: Depletion of the resource, evident for years, was one of the first concerns of the new state government. In February 1959, one of the first acts of the new state legislature was to outlaw fish traps.

As well as earning his salary running the Loring cannery, making profits off the general store in Loring, and earning money on the side as the community's postmaster, the enterprising Heckman made many thousands of dollars off his invention. The Heckman Fish Trap Co. brought in an average of $6,000 a year for 17 years, until the trap patent expired. Among other things, Heckman invested in the fledgling community of Ketchikan. At the turn of the century, he invested in a store in Ketchikan, put W.A. Bryant in charge, and the J.R. Heckman & Co. store became so profitable that he never had to invest any more money in it. Almost 100 years later, although Heckman's

The Fortmann hatchery, built in 1901 on nearby Heckman Lake, was once the world's largest and most expensive hatchery operating with a live-in crew and supplies carried over from the cannery. (Tongass Historical Museum Collection)

store itself is no longer, a block of stores in downtown Ketchikan still bears his name. Heckman was a director of Ketchikan's Miners & Merchants Bank at its beginning in 1906, and was its president for many years. Heckman was a member of the International Order of Odd Fellows, Eagles, Elks, Improved Order of Redmen, Pioneers of Alaska, Scottish Rite Masons, Commandry and Shrine and Order of the Eastern Star. In his spare time, he ran for and was elected to the Territorial House of Representatives (one term) and Territorial Senate (two terms). He was also a director of the National Bank of Commerce in Seattle, and had interests in dozens of other enterprises. No

slouch in the family department either, Heckman married Marie C. Capp of San Francisco in 1893. They had 10 children: five daughters and five sons. When his funeral was held in 1939, most of the businesses in Ketchikan closed. The Masonic Lodge had to open all three floors to accommodate the crowds, and pipe in the funeral service to the first and third floors through loudspeakers.

Hatchery

To rebuild a rapidly depleting resource, a new federal law passed in 1900 required those who caught salmon in Alaska waters to build and run hatcheries near their fisheries operations. They had to produce four times as many salmon as the number of mature salmon they took the previous season. Two years later, the law was amended to require the replacement of 10 times as many salmon as had been taken.

APA responded to the federal legislation by building the

world's largest and most expensive hatchery on Heckman Lake, eight miles inland from Loring, in 1901. Built of logs and hand-hewn shakes, the hatchery was in effect a small town, with two main hatchery buildings, a sawmill, a barn housing cows, calves, chickens, pigs and rabbits, and low sheds for drying wood. A crew of men and women lived at the hatchery for the season.

In the spring when the supplies came in, the crew lived in a bunkhouse called "the smokehouse," which contained the only telephone between the Loring cannery and the hatchery. Supplies loaded onto skiffs were transported up through the rapids and across the lagoon, unloaded from the skiffs and loaded onto a tramcar drawn by a mule to the landing on Jordan Lake. From there, they were ferried across to a warehouse, loaded aboard another tramcar on which they made the steep climb to the hatchery lake, and were then ferried across to the hatchery. Trail maintenance was a major chore, especially for the crew that worked through the winter. When the lakes were frozen over and hatchery worker Milton Orton had to bring in the Christmas mail sacks, woe be to the crew that didn't keep the trail in good shape.

Hatchery workers formed a community of their own. Bountiful gardens flourished, livestock grazed. Crew members worked hard all day and played at night. People would rush to the boiler room on Saturday nights to bathe and launder their clothes and get ready for a party. Dances on Saturday nights and midweek, with jazz records on the old phonograph, moonlight clambakes complete with bootleg liquor, late-night games of pool, cribbage and mah-jongg in the mess hall, sportfishing, duck hunting, boat racing — adventurers from all over the world worked seven days a week together during the fishing season and got to know each other even better in the evenings.

In 1927, a way of life ended when the Fortmann hatchery, named for the president of APA, was shut down. The federal law mandating canners to maintain hatcheries had been amended to make hatcheries voluntary. 1927 had been a bad season for the Alaska fishing industry; the APA cannery at Loring packed a paltry number of cases. Unwilling to abandon the good life they

had known, the hatchery's cook, Kate McKay, and Milton Orton married and stayed on to caretake the hatchery. They eventually homesteaded closer to the smokehouse, creating a wilderness ranch with wonderful gardens, and hunted, trapped, wrote — in short, did everything they could to keep living on what today is termed "Orton Ranch."

The Stewarts and the Stacks

In the 1800s, a group of Tsimshian Indians had formed an utopian Christian community at Metlakatla, B.C., under the leadership of the Rev. William Duncan. When Duncan had a

July 1, 1909, the Teal *tugs 14 skiffs between Loring's cannery and the Fortmann hatchery at Heckman Lake. All supplies for hatchery workers were shipped on the skiffs, then loaded onto tramcars pulled by mules and ferried across the lake to make the eight mile trek. (Tongass Historical Museum Collection #73.3.16.228)*

falling out with his church hierarchy, he and a group of his followers decided to form a new community. After receiving permission from the Tlingit tribe who had traditional rights to Annette Island, the Tsimshian headed north to settle on Annette.

In 1887, Mariah Stewart and her family left Old Metlakatla to head north, but had their own disagreements with the Rev. Duncan. So she and her family settled in Loring instead. Three years later, Dick Stack came north to rebuild the Loring cannery after it had been severely damaged by fire. Mariah must have enjoyed the company of Dick Stack, with his booming voice and good nature, for they soon were engaged to be married. This was not to the Rev. Duncan's liking. So strong were his beliefs that Natives and whites should not intermarry that he absolutely refused to perform the ceremony. Mariah and Dick had to turn elsewhere for their wedding. But they persevered, for by August 1890, they are listed in the census as husband and wife. And a new member of the Loring community, a baby named William Stack, is listed right after them. Soon they were joined by more Stacks, as Mariah and Dick's family increased.

Mariah's brother, Capt. William Stewart, salvaged lumber from the *Ancon*, a sidewheel steamer carrying noted artist Albert Bierstadt and Colorado Gov. Alva Adams and his family to Loring as tourists when it wrecked on a reef just a few feet out from the Loring dock in 1889. Stewart built a sturdy home from the lumber, which he later sold to Con Giebel, Loring photographer and storekeeper, who in turn sold it to Mariah's daughter, Margaret, and her new husband, Sixten Johanson, for $100. They lived many happy years in the "Ancon House." A little more than a century after it was built, the Ancon House, in disrepair, was burned down.

School

In 1900, the federal government made education mandatory for all Alaska school-age children. Each morning of the academic year between 21 and 28 young Loring residents trooped to the little school.

Born in 1914, Tom Stack, Mariah and Dick's youngest son, only attended the Loring school for two years. The school closed in 1921, and the rest of his education had to be informal. Tom had the run of the village, and delighted in the time of year when the square-rigged sailing ships came in to port, took down their sails, and docked for the season. His mother made home brew, and young Tom sold it to sailors. His father, skipper of the tug *Novelty*, would meet the ships at Chacon, on Prince of Wales Island, and tow them into port. Tom Stack joined the APA work force at age 16 as a cannery hand, and worked at the cannery until it closed. Today, he makes his home in Ketchikan.

One of Tom's schoolmates and fellow Ketchikan elder who also only had the opportunity to attend Loring school for a few years was Bruce Johnstone, who moved to Loring in 1919 at age 10. Loring at that time surpassed Ketchikan in size, with 300 residents. In the summers, Johnstone's family handlogged. In the winter, they hunted, prospected and trapped, and traded their meat and furs to the townfolk for the goods they needed. The year before they moved to Loring, 9-year-old Bruce and his sister had earned money for the family by hunting bears and selling their skulls to the Smithsonian for $45 each.

The Silver Horde

Loring was winding down in 1930. With the hatchery idle and APA closing down its canning operations in other parts of Southeast, the future did not look promising. Then the town livened up from an unexpected source: Hollywood. R.K.O. Studios planned to film a new version of Rex Beach's novel, *The Silver Horde* (1909), a "talking" picture, starring Evelyn Brent, Louis Wolheim, Raymond Hatton, Gavin Gordon, Ivan Lenion and debuting Joel McCrae. Arch MacDonald, manager of the Liberty Theatre in Ketchikan, lobbied intensively to convince the producers to film the movie in and around Ketchikan.

In July 1930, the Alaska Line steamer *Lakina* headed north with more than 60 members of the R.K.O. film company, and 150 Asian cannery workers. R.K.O. shot some of the movie aboard the S.S. *Lakina* with the captain and crew, and, once filming began on site, shot footage of their fellow passengers, the Asian cannery hands, at work. Loring was the main site for filming, with some scenes shot at Ward Cove and Mud Bay.

About 25 miles northwest of Loring, the tiny settlement of Meyers Chuck is tucked into the tip of the Cleveland Peninsula. (Steve McCutcheon)

Ketchikan and Loring buzzed with excitement and the economic boost. R.K.O. chartered boats, scows and a Washington Airways plane for transporting crew and 50 tons of equipment to Loring. Every morning at 6:25 a.m., the janitor at the Elks' Lodge heard Joel McCrae and Raymond Hatton coming down Dock St. singing at the top of their lungs on their way to board their plane for Loring. Evelyn Brent didn't like the color of her room at the Gilmore, so the hotel had it repainted in pink. The crew returned to Ketchikan each night to eat up a storm at the Blue Fox Cafe.

On July 21, the Elks threw a party for the film crew at the Redmen's Hall in Ketchikan. The R.K.O. crew departed from the Alaska Steamship dock in Ketchikan the next evening, as hundreds of local people bid them farewell. Crowds turned out to see the world premiere of *The Silver Horde*, shown at Arch MacDonald's Liberty Theatre on Nov. 7, 1930.

Downsizing in Loring

By the time the world saw Loring in *The Silver Horde*, the community was in deep trouble. The closing of the Fortmann hatchery in 1927 foreshadowed the end of the boomtown. APA was finding its Southeast operations less and less profitable. They had already closed their Chilkat and Point Highfield plants, near Haines and on Wrangell Island respectively, when the decision was made to shut down operations in Loring. The 1930 pack was the Loring cannery's last.

The cannery building and its equipment were dismantled. Most people said goodbye to friends and fellow workers, and never returned. A few hardy souls stayed on.

Milton and Kate Orton and their sons stayed on for many years. Milton died while running his trapline in 1950, and when David Orton was killed in a logging accident three years later, Kate's family arrived and helped Kate and her other son pack up and depart Loring. Tom Stack met Florence Ebena in Metlakatla. They married in 1940, the year Dick Stack died, and moved to Loring two years later. A few other people associated with APA operations in Loring stayed on, doing whatever they could to earn a living that would allow them to stay in "paradise," and with the years, a few newcomers joined the small community. Noted Alaska author Margaret Bell Wiks made Loring her home for many years.

Today, the community has shrunk to about 11 homes, most of which are weekend or summer residences. Sealaska, the Southeast Native regional corporation, owns the land the cannery formerly occupied. The First Baptist Church owns the old Orton Ranch, and runs an annual Bible camp there. The Stack family maintains a presence in the tiny community. And the wind through the trees still carries the echoes of the women, men and children who lived, laughed, worked and played in Loring, Alaska, when it was in its glory. ▮

The Communities of Prince of Wales

By Kerre Martineau

With more than 2,200 square miles of land and 990 miles of coastline, Prince of Wales Island ranks as the third largest island in the nation after Hawaii and Kodiak. Its population of 6,300 includes Haidas, Tlingits and non-Natives in 28 incorporated and unincorporated communities.

Nearly one-third of the island's population lives in Craig, a predominately non-Native town with the most diverse economy on the island. Residents here participate in commercial fishing and processing, logging, local government and services and a growing tourism industry.

Smaller island communities, such as Coffman Cove, Kasaan and Port Protection, are primarily single-industry settlements. Coffman Cove began as a logging camp in the 1970s and now has a population of nearly 200, most of whom work in the logging industry or in support businesses. Kasaan, Tlingit for "beautiful city by the sea," also began with the logging industry.

More than 200 years ago, Haidas came to Prince of Wales from the Queen Charlotte Islands in British Columbia and settled at what is now Old Kasaan. Then in the 1880s, they moved across the bay to present-day Kasaan for jobs at its new sawmill. In 1996 Kasaan had a reported population of 45.

Port Protection's seasonal population of 55 in winter and up to 70 in summer mostly consists of fishing families. A small trading post operates in Port Protection as a stop for local charter floatplane service and fresh-fish sales.

Exploitation of Prince of Wales began in 1867 with the discovery of copper near Kasaan, and soon after gold and marble mining began. As the mining boom died down, the fishing industry took over the island, first with commercial fishing for salmon then with the opening of a cannery in Klawock. Fishing and logging operations now share the island's economy.

Prior to 1951, when logging began on the island, no usable roads existed between the communities. Currently, travelers have access to more than 1,400 miles of old logging roads, some of which are paved, such as between Hollis, Klawock and Craig.

FACING PAGE: *Most communities on the island are waterfront settlements with a strong dependence on and connection to surrounding waters. Some businesses and homes, like this restaurant in Craig, are actually built over the water on pilings. (Sharon Brosamle)*

ABOVE: *Acidic runoff water from Southeast's muskeg plants erodes the limestone and carves caves and sinkholes underneath the island's surface. Many caves on Prince of Wales have been mapped by volunteers and are accessible to the public, but cave walls and features are fragile and should not be handled or disturbed. (Hall Anderson)*

RIGHT: *Moss and old-growth are common features of Alaska's Southeast forests. Moderate temperatures and average annual rainfall of 60 to 200 inches support this rain forest-type environment filled with Sitka spruce and western hemlock. (Craig J. Flatten)*

Other roads are still gravel, and the road system does not extend to every community on the island. The latest addition to the network, Kasaan, was connected in 1996. Some smaller settlements on southern Prince of Wales, for example Chomly, Dolomi and Klinkwan, are accessible only by boat or floatplane.

Hollis maintains the island's dock for the Alaska Marine Highway System, which provides ferry service across Clarence Strait to Ketchikan. Round trips are scheduled one to five times per week in winter and seven times per week during peak summer travel. Several air carriers provide airplane access to communities on the island and most areas have public docks for private boats and planes.

Visitors to Prince of Wales Island can find lodges and motels in most larger communities and bed and breakfasts in many smaller settlements. Indoor plumbing is available in a majority of residences and businesses in the major cities and most communities are connected to surface water sources. Electricity is generated by diesel and widely available from several power companies on the island; however, most homes are heated with stove oil, wood or propane to avoid high electric rates. In 1995, a new hydroelectric project as a subsidiary of Alaska Power & Telephone Co. was dedicated at Black Bear Lake and currently serves Craig, Klawock and surrounding areas. Energy produced at the facility is calculated to save approximately 70,000 barrels of oil annually.

Alaska Rural Communication Service (ARCS) provides television reception for local stations and cable service is available through community cable providers. Private satellite dishes at some homes allow viewers access to DIRECTV programming.

The U.S. Forest Service controls much of the island's land and has designated certain areas for recreational use. Forest Service offices at Craig and Thorne Bay offer cabins and campsites throughout the island, all with access to prime salmon fishing. Salmon derbies held annually at Thorne Bay and Craig give all a chance to walk away with prizes and trophies for big catches.

LEFT: *Honker Divide, one of the last uncut drainages on Prince of Wales Island, is the focus of logging versus wildlife/old-growth forest debates. (Craig J. Flatten)*

BELOW: *Visitors come from miles around to fish the waters of Prince of Wales in search of prize-winning salmon and halibut. Annual derbies at Craig and Thorne Bay reward the most successful fishermen with gifts and cash awards. (Roy Corral)*

Craig

Craig, originally named Fish Egg for the abundant herring eggs in nearby waters, began as a temporary fishing camp for Tlingit Indians. Each spring they would travel to the camp from miles around to collect herring eggs from nearby waters. In 1907, entrepreneur Craig Millar built a mild-cure salmon packing plant on the site and by 1911, a cold storage facility, permanent saltery and more than two dozen homes were built. Fish Egg became known as Craig and incorporated as a first-class city in 1922.

In 1912, Lindenberger Packing Co. built a salmon cannery and E.M. Streeter moved in with the city's first sawmill to

Craig actually spans two islands connected by a short causeway. As the largest city on Prince of Wales Island, Craig offers all necessary services to visitors and island residents. (Terry Fifield)

launch Craig's second largest industry. Craig's population, at 1,946 in 1996 according to state records, expanded throughout the 1930s as more and more people moved to the island in search of employment. During summer months, this population may double or even triple with construction, logging and fishing seasonal workers in town. Currently, fishing is still the city's primary industry, with timber harvesting a close second. However, because of excellent sportfishing in the area, the improved island road system and recent renovations to nearby Klawock's airstrip, tourism is fast becoming an important industry for Craig.

Several new facilities have been built, and many more are being planned in Craig to support its growing population and tourism. Attracting much attention, especially in winter, is the Craig Aquatic Center, featuring an indoor pool, fitness room, sauna and spa. Since it opened in January 1996, more than 150 people have visited the center each day, including busloads of children from other island communities. A bond issue supported the center's construction, while a 1 percent increase in the city sales tax finances its operation.

To increase summertime recreation, the city built a second baseball field at the ballpark and is planning to expand the walking paths and bike trails around the park. Plans for expansion in the city include a new water treatment facility and industrial park. The water treatment facility will include more pump stations to reach recently developed residential areas of town not served by the current facility. Many other businesses will have the opportunity to expand at the new industrial park, a 20-year project that is expected to bring more businesses and jobs to Craig.

BELOW: *Spruce grouse inhabit much of the island, but stay well camouflaged in the thick underbrush of the forests. Other wildlife on the island includes Sitka black-tailed deer and black bears. The grouse is a member of a recently recognized distinct subspecies that is the only temperate rain forest spruce grouse subspecies. These birds occur only on Prince of Wales and adjacent islands. (Craig J. Flatten)*

BELOW RIGHT: *Commercial and private fishing boats can be seen lining the docks at most communities on the island. Craig has two small-boat harbors for fishing fleets and cargo barge access for shipping and receiving supplies. (Staff)*

FACING PAGE: *At Whale Pass on north Prince of Wales Island, fishing can be both productive and peaceful. With so many creeks, rivers, bays and beaches in and around the island, it isn't difficult to find a quiet spot with plenty of fish. (Harry M. Walker)*

RIGHT: *The abundance of fish in island waterways makes a suitable habitat for Southeast's black bear population, often a target of big game hunters. As new roads are opened, hunters have access to animal populations that have little experience with people. The roads also provide poachers with opportunities to kill unwary animals. (Sharon Brosamle)*

The town's local Native organization, Shaan-Seet Inc., operates many businesses including a logging company, hotel, trailer park and a gravel business that sells construction and fill material. Since 1970, Shaan-Seet Inc. has been a presence in Craig providing necessary services and approximately 100 jobs for area residents. In recent years however, island corporations have seen a decline in logging and fishing businesses and an increasing interest in mining. In response, Shaan-Seet, Inc. is now considering mining limestone on Prince of Wales Island.

Residents and tourists are kept entertained year-round with various festivals and activities. At Christmastime, fishing boats, decked in holiday lights, parade through the bay. On the Fourth of July, residents decorate their land-dwelling vehicles and parade through town, then everyone gathers at the city ballpark to sample offerings from food and arts and crafts booths and watch the fireworks show.

Celebrating Craig's heritage, the annual Fish Egg Festival draws everyone outside to enjoy live music, games and races for children and adults, and food and arts and crafts displays. A little more down to business is the Trade Show, sponsored by the Prince of Wales Chamber of Commerce. Held each year at the Craig city gym, the show gives business owners a chance to display their wares and explain their services to island residents.

Sportfishing is the main draw for Craig's tourists. Through-out the year, several species of fish are available including halibut, salmon, red snapper, steelhead and rainbow trout, rockfish and cod. Each July, winners of the Craig-Klawock King Salmon Derby receive prizes for their best catches. Approximately 600 people participate in the derby and compete for cash and prizes worth more than $25,000, with the top winner receiving a new boat, motor and trailer.

As the service center for the island, Craig offers many facilities for visitors to Prince of Wales. A new state-owned seaplane base and U.S. Coast Guard heliport are in Craig and a newly renovated airport is just seven miles down the road in Klawock. Cargo barges call at Craig's docks in the summer bringing supplies from the mainland, while year-round ship-ments arrive from the Old Chilkat dock at Hollis, 30 miles away on the island road system. Craig offers all necessary services such as fuel, car repairs, car rentals, accommodations and restaurants. Even Burger King has moved to the island and made its home in this tiny metropolis.

Klawock

Klawock began as a summer fishing camp for the Tahn-da-quan Indians of Moira Sound, who had lived full-time on the west coast of the island before moving their primary winter camp to Moira Sound on south Prince of Wales. According to William L. Paul Sr. in *The Alaska Journal*, Klawock is named for a Tahn-da-quan man who moved his family from the camp

at Moira Sound back to the original site on the west side of Prince of Wales Island. The site became known by the man's name, Kloo-wah, then after many spelling variations, changed to Klawock when the city incorporated in 1929.

Since its beginning as a part-time fishing camp, Klawock has depended heavily on fish for the bulk of its economy and primary subsistence food. In 1868, George Hamilton opened a trading post and salmon saltery here. Ten years later he sold it to Sisson, Wallace and Co. of San Francisco, who built the first Alaska salmon cannery on the site. The cannery operated primarily with local labor, but because of the seasonality of salmon harvests, Klawock's population fluctuated greatly from winter to summer with workers moving away during off seasons to find other work. To maintain operations, federal funding was awarded to the cannery in 1934 with the stipulation that the city be kept free of liquor. State records listed Klawock's population at 759 in 1996.

Although cannery operations ceased in the 1980s, the state Klawock River hatchery, operated by the non-profit Prince of Wales Hatchery Association Inc., continues to enhance the local fish population, and several residents still hold commercial fishing permits. Recently, logging has taken over as the primary economy with Viking Lumber Co. a large employer in the area. The city also plans to broaden its economy with a new cold storage plant and increased tourism promotion.

With docks for floatplanes and a paved airstrip for small wheeled aircraft, Klawock already hosts many visitors from

LEFT: *William Demmert and son Phillip show off their catch during a fishing break on Prince of Wales Island in the summer of 1969. At the time, Demmert was chief administrator of Klawock public schools. Later he became commissioner of education under former Gov. Steve Cowper. (Bill Foster)*

FACING PAGE: *Klawock's totem park, containing 21 totems from the abandoned village of Tuxekan, stands on a hill overlooking the town and cannery. (Roy Corral)*

Ketchikan. However, for those preferring to travel on land, the city is also connected to other Prince of Wales communities via the island road system and is a 24-mile drive from the ferry terminal at Hollis.

No matter how they arrive, locals and tourists alike enjoy canoeing and boating on Klawock Lake, fishing for salmon and steelhead trout on Klawock River and hunting deer and black bear inland. Another draw is the totem park made up of restored original and replicated totems from the abandoned village of Tuxekan and newly renovated with funds from the Rural Development Assistance Agency. Arranged in a park overlooking the city, the totems stand in remembrance of the Tlingit's

BELOW: *Next to fishing, logging is the largest industry on Prince of Wales Island. Nearly 85 percent of the island is considered part of the Tongass National Forest and managed by the U.S. Forest Service. (Roy Corral)*

RIGHT: *Robert Peratrovich Sr., early Klawock entrepreneur, stands in the doorway of his store in 1969. Peratrovich operated the first movie theater, power plant and water system in Klawock; he died in 1972 at age 88. (Bill Foster)*

original Native village. Also under construction are a visitor's center, museum and totem storage facility.

Each year, Alaska Native Brotherhood and Sisterhood sponsor the Elizabeth Peratrovich Celebration in Klawock. Peratrovich, a Tlingit, fought for Native rights in Alaska. As Grand President of Alaska Native Sisterhood, she spoke before the territorial Senate in 1945 lobbying for passage of Alaska Territory's Anti-Discrimination Act. The bill passed the Senate and was signed on Feb. 16, 1945. Alaska now recog-nizes Feb. 16 as Elizabeth Peratrovich Day. Klawock's annual celebration usually includes a potluck dinner, a parade and presentations by elders and youths about Native rights issues.

As with most other small communities, Klawock focuses much attention on its children. The town rallies around the school basketball and volleyball teams with large turnouts at local games. Additionally, plans are currently under way to reopen the youth center that closed due to lack of funding. Pool tables, video games, televisions and other activities will again be available to all school-age children. In the meantime, the school gymnasium is open three evenings a week as a place the youngsters can play games or just socialize.

Currently, the city offers accommodations, hunting and fishing charter services, food and sporting goods stores, repair shops and gas stations. However, some facilities and businesses in Klawock have closed in recent years. Karen Clark, municipal clerk, attributes much of the problem to high electric rates. She claims that Tlingit-Haida Regional Electrical Authority's rates in Klawock are nearly twice as high as rates in Craig, which is supplied by Alaska Power and Telephone Co. THREA purchases power at wholesale rates and resells it to Klawock residents at a substantial markup. Therefore, Craig, just seven miles down the road, is the new home for many shops and services.

This juvenile female northern goshawk is part of a population on Prince of Wales Island that has been studied comprehensively in recent years because extensive logging has influenced the goshawk's habitat. (Craig J. Flatten)

Thorne Bay

Thorne Bay, one of Alaska's newest second-class cities, began as a logging camp like many other island communities. In 1960, Thorne Bay was home to a floating logging camp. Quickly, the logging industry grew and the camp moved on shore. When Ketchikan Pulp Co. ceased operations at Hollis in 1962, Thorne Bay provided a barge terminal, log sort yard and a larger camp to house the relocated company.

Thorne Bay was originally named in 1891 for Frank Manley Thorn, then superintendent of the U.S. Coast & Geodetic Survey. The difference in spelling occurred as an error in the first publication of the bay's name and has remained the city's official name ever since.

The once-tiny logging camp boasted a population of 650 in 1996. Most residents work for logging companies and the U.S. Forest Service, although some work in local service trades and for the municipal government. In 1974, Thorne Bay was added to the island road system via an unpaved road from Klawock. Although the city is more water-travel than land-travel oriented, the new road has enabled visitors off the ferry to enjoy Thorne Bay's beautiful scenery and plentiful salmon sportfishing.

Located on an inlet off Clarence Strait, Thorne Bay receives many visitors by boat and floatplane from Ketchikan. A seaplane base and small-boat harbor are available for public use. Many tourists and locals migrate here during summer to enjoy canoeing, kayaking, sailing and waterskiing.

Each year Thorne Bay hosts its annual Thorne Bay Salmon Derby and the Prince of Wales Island Fair and Logging Show. May through July 1997 marks the 37th annual salmon derby with more than 250 participants expected. Last year, Bill Welton

ABOVE LEFT: *A house in Thorne Bay reflects the resourceful and whimsical nature of many Alaskans. (Diane Stittgen)*

LEFT: *Thorne Bay, population 650, is nestled along the shore of a bay with the same name on the east coast of Prince of Wales Island. (John Wolon)*

Hydaburg's cannery supports most of the town's residents during fishing season. At other times of the year, Hydaburg's second largest industry, logging, and subsistence hunting and fishing supplement the Haidas' incomes. (Don Cornelius)

of Thorne Bay caught the grand prize winner, a 40-pound king salmon, and went home with a new 16-foot skiff and 40-horsepower outboard motor. A special derby for children age 15 and younger allows the whole family to participate in the fun.

The Island Fair and Logging Show, sponsored by the Prince of Wales Chamber of Commerce each July, invites all Alaska residents to participate. During this weekend, children and adults enter creations in a range of exhibits from canned goods and cookies to clothing and jewelry. At the logging show, men and women demonstrate their skills and compete for awards and the title of All-Around Logger. Events include speed climbing, ax throwing, power saw bucking and a hooktenders pimp race. The latter requires two people, one to carry a cable up a pole (the hooktender) and the other (the pimp) to hoist a block that is wrapped with the cable and remains suspended from the pole. Events for women only include the rolling pin toss, hammer over-head throw and pole walk.

When not practicing for the next logging show, Thorne Bay residents can usually be found at city school functions, such as basketball games and wrestling meets. City council meetings also draw a large crowd. Locals enjoy hunting, fishing and hiking in the area. And, as if all that were not enough, Karen Petersen, assistant city clerk for Thorne Bay, emphatically adds, "once a month we have bunco night!"

For visitors, the city offers limited accommodations and a restaurant. Thorne Bay Health Clinic, built in 1995, is owned and operated by the city. General merchandise stores, car and boat repair and various fuel supply outlets are also available.

Hydaburg

Hydaburg, 1996 population 406, is the largest Native village on Prince of Wales and the largest Haida village in Alaska.

In 1911, three Haida villages (Sukkwan, Klinkwan and Howkan) joined together to form Hydaburg and to start a centralized school for their children. This early community was recognized by the government as an Indian reservation and soon a school was built. However, at the request of the residents in 1926, the government restored Hydaburg's land to its original status as part of Tongass National Forest, with a small portion of the land set aside for the townsite. Approximately 15 years later, Hydaburg incorporated as a first-class city and was the site for the first salmon processing plant on the island. Hydaburg Cooperative Association currently maintains the plant.

As a supplement to salmon processing, Hydaburg is working with Seaplus Marketing from Canada to establish a small specialty seafood processing plant, scheduled to open in 1997 and to process shrimp. Formerly, a floating shrimp processor operated off the coast of Hydaburg, but now fishermen take their catch elsewhere for processing. Having the new plant in town should boost Hydaburg's economy.

Although commercial fishing for salmon, shrimp and halibut is the primary industry for Hydaburg, the Haida still depend heavily on subsistence fishing and hunting. Logging, the town's second largest industry, also supports many of its residents. Haida Corp. controls a large timber sorting yard and storage facility, which are now leased to Sealaska Corp., the Native regional corporation for Southeast. Although timber harvesting has been on hold in the area since 1985 because of a decline in the market, Sealaska Corp. still retains interest in further developing the industry.

As the principal community of Haida Indians in Southeast,

Hydaburg maintains a strong connection to its cultural heritage. Haida originated from the Queen Charlotte island group in British Columbia and only began to migrate to Alaska's Southeast in the past 200 years. Once arriving on Prince of Wales Island, the Haida formed several small villages, the largest of them being Sukkwan, Klinkwan and Howkan. Each village,

BELOW: *Hydaburg elder Sylvester Peele displays traditional Haida dress. Hydaburg, Alaska's largest Haida village, had a population of 406 in 1996. (Roy Corral)*

RIGHT: *Totems from Klinkwan, Sukkwan and Howkan stand in a Hydaburg park in remembrance of the former home villages of the town's residents. (Don Pitcher)*

while following general Haida customs, also established its own individuality. This is best seen in the difference in totem designs among the villages. After the three combined to form Hydaburg, residents transplanted and reconstructed totems from each of the original villages. In the 1930s, the Civilian Conservation Corps restored the totems and created a totem park for them in town.

Children of Hydaburg also take an active role in maintaining their city's cultural heritage with an annual school-sponsored Haida Day. On Haida Day, all members of the town are invited

Among the smaller logging camps on Prince of Wales Island is Coffman Cove on the island's northeast shore. The community is named for Naval Lt. DeWitt Coffman, who sailed with Lt. Cmdr. A.S. Snow on a cruise through the area in 1886. (John Wolon)

to view various Native artworks produced by the children.

Doug Mathena, mayor of Hydaburg, says that education and the children are his top priorities while in office. In support of this, the town has recently opened its youth center, a project that has been under way for years. At the youth center, school-age children can play games like pool, darts, board games and foos ball. Mathena insists that no video games will be placed at the center. He intends the center to be "recreational and

Prince of Wales and some other islands in southern Southeast have been heavily logged, with much of the timber going to supply the pulp mill and sawmill at Ketchikan. Here a barge loaded with chips from Louisiana Pacific's Annette Hemlock Mill comes into the pulp mill at Ward Cove. During the pulp-making process, the chips are mixed with other wood, cooked, bleached, dried and formed into 20-ton jumbo rolls. The rolls are put onto a cutter that cuts them into bales of a size specified by the customer. The bales usually weigh about 440 pounds. They are wrapped with wire and loaded by longshoremen onto ships for transport to market. (John Wolon)

educational, promoting cooperation amongst the kids." Alaska State Troopers donated a computer to the youth center and several more are scheduled to be purchased. Also in the plans is a talking circle, suggested by the children, for the youngsters to talk to each other about current issues affecting them. Mathena hopes the youth center will be a long-running success, but warns that without continued support from the community, the donation-funded center will have to close.

While the youth center is strictly for school-age children, adults can find entertainment at the local churches where game nights are held. In the past, bingo and pull-tabs have also been available. Of course, the Fourth of July celebrations always draw a large crowd. Each year, the town puts on an Independence Day carnival.

Most visitors are attracted to Hydaburg by its reputation for excellent salmon fishing. As with the other major communities on the island, Hydaburg can be reached by boat, plane or car. A state-owned seaplane base can be approached by way of a federally designated route regularly used by charter flights from Ketchikan. A small-boat harbor and dock are available as well as a home port for large commercial fishing fleets. Regularly scheduled barges deliver supplies and cargo from Seattle; other deliveries are made by state ferry and trucked into Hydaburg, 36 miles southwest of the dock at Hollis.

Hydaburg offers its visitors restaurants and lodging. Several specialty stores, grocery stores, charter services and gas stations are also available. However, as a dry community, no liquor sales are permitted within the city.

Hollis

While other areas of the island flourished with the rise of fishing and logging industries, discovery of gold at the turn of the century brought people flocking to Hollis. Originally a camp for the Cracker Jack Mine in the 1890s, the settlement was named Hollis City after its founder and part owner of the mine, A. Hollis White. Located on a major water route through the island and close to several mines in the area, Hollis soon became a gold-mining boomtown. However, the boom was short-lived and quickly petered out after it began in the early 1900s.

Nearly 50 years after the gold-mining era, Hollis was transformed into a logging community. In the 1950s, the U.S. Forest Service awarded a 50-year logging contract to Ketchikan Pulp Co., which used Hollis as its first operating base. The camp served all logging operations on Prince of Wales until 1962, when logging was completed in the Harris River valley near Hollis. Camp buildings were then packed onto barges and moved to Thorne Bay.

Currently, Hollis depends on the Alaska Marine Highway ferry system. Having the only ferry terminal on the island and the only connection from outside to the Prince of Wales Island road system, Hollis is host to a regular captive audience making the two hour and 45 minute commute from Ketchikan. For non-ferry traffic, Hollis also maintains docks for floatplanes and small boats. Old logging roads, some paved, provide access to other communities on the island.

In 1996 the Alaska Department of Labor estimated Hollis' population at 106, down from approximately 1,000 during gold-mining days. Permanent settlement at this community was made possible through recent government land sales.

Those who live in Hollis enjoy its solitude and have no current plans for expansion. Bill MacCannell of the *Island News* in Thorne Bay lived in Hollis during the land sales and says that people live there "because they don't want to live in the mainstream, they want to get away from the rush." Most residents hunt and fish and receive their income from work on the ferry system and logging support services on the island. Social activities in town revolve around the small school and its functions. All other activities and services require travel to another city on the island or across Clarence Strait to Ketchikan.

Although many of Hollis' facilities are government-owned or regulated, such as the seaplane base, the state ferry system and the U.S. Forest Service, Hollis itself eschews central government. Instead it is organized by a non-profit community council. As an unincorporated community, Hollis receives state money that

Several miles north of Klawock off Tuxekan Passage is Naukati Bay and the logging community of the same name. (John Wolon)

the community directs to various projects such as the school library and emergency medical services. Even the post office, established in 1901 for the growing population of the gold-mining days, ceased its operations in 1942. Mail is now brought over in pouches from Ketchikan and distributed by community members.

Visitors to Hollis enjoy good salmon and trout fishing in area waters, but will not find many public amenities awaiting them. No accommodations, grocery stores, restaurants or gas stations are available in the tiny settlement. The closest location for visitor facilities is 25 miles west down a paved road to Klawock, then another seven miles on to Craig. However, at the Hollis School a telephone is available for public use. ∎

Metlakatla

By Kerre Martineau

A nearby waterfall, accessible beaches and a protected bay first drew the Tsimshians to settle at what they called New Metlakatla on Annette Island. More than 100 years later, this predominately Native community still thrives on local resources from the waters that attracted them there.

In the mid-1800s, 400 Tsimshian Indians left their homeland in Fort Simpson, B.C., in search of religious freedom. This group, led by Scottish priest Father William Duncan, settled at Old Metlakatla near Prince Rupert, B.C., but 20 years after building their model community, the Anglican Church replaced Duncan. He left in 1887, followed by a small group of loyal worshippers, to settle in a deserted Tlingit village on Annette Island. President Grover Cleveland granted the land to the group and Congress declared it a federal Indian reservation in 1891.

Today, Annette Island remains the only federal reservation in Alaska for indigenous people. Under their 1891 charter, Annette Island's Tsimshian community maintains control of all 86,000 acres of land on the island and the waters within 3,000 feet of shore. They voted down participation in the Alaska Native Claims Settlement Act of 1971, which awarded village corporations 23,000 acres of land. Most of the island's inhabitants live in Metlakatla, population 1,603, which is 84 percent Native according to recent state surveys.

Living in a small island community, residents of Metlakatla are a close-knit group. Most members of the community turn out for island activities such as sporting events at the schools or dancing and basket-weaving at the longhouse, a tribal community center used for traditional Tsimshian gatherings. Another frequent gathering place is the Lepquinum (Tsimshian for "our own") Activity Center operated by the island school district. Center facilities and programs include a swimming pool, sauna, exercise room, art rooms and University of Alaska Southeast outreach classes.

Metlakatla functions as a traditional Tsimshian community with fishing and logging its primary industries. Due to the

FACING PAGE: *More than 60 residents of Metlakatla currently hold commercial fishing permits and help stock the community cannery. Tsimshian residents have exclusive rights to all waters within 3,000 feet of the island because of their 1891 charter from Congress. (Jerry Jordan)*

The original church built by the Rev. William Duncan and his followers in 1887 burned to the ground in 1948. Volunteers later built this replica and dedicated it the William Duncan Memorial Church. (Jerry Jordan)

island's reservation status, its companies do not fall under state or federal jurisdiction, therefore certain exceptions to government laws and regulations are granted to the Tsimshians. The community regulates all commercial fishing in the waters surrounding the island, and is the only organization in the state allowed to operate floating fish traps commercially. Fish traps were outlawed in 1959, when Alaska became a state, because they proved too efficient and depleted the natural salmon supply. To supplement their incomes, many of the Tsimshian also participate in subsistence hunting and fishing.

Also because of its status as an Indian reservation, the Tsimshian's government proceedings are exempt from federal or state control. Metlakatla Indian Community operates the island's Tribal Court, Tribal Juvenile Court and Tribal Appellate Court, which hear all legal proceedings for the community.

Local companies provide most utilities. Metlakatla Power & Light operates the hydroelectric facilities maintaining the water system and supplying electricity to the island. According to the 1990 census, all homes in Metlakatla have indoor plumbing and are connected to the central water system. Alaska Rural Communication Service (ARCS) provides most television programming; however, some Canadian stations send programming via translators and cable television is widely available from the community-owned cable station.

Metlakatla Indian Community, which owns many businesses in town, remains the largest employer on the island. Currently, the community operates Annette Island Medical Clinic; Annette Island Packing Co., consisting of a cold storage unit and salmon cannery; the airport; several local services and a salmon hatchery on Tamgass Bay, which replenishes the natural supplies of five salmon species.

During World War II, the U.S. Army constructed an air base a few miles from Metlakatla and the Coast Guard also kept a base nearby. Amphibious planes used the bases for some time after the war, shuttling tourists to Metlakatla from Ketchikan. However, all operations at the bases have since ceased. Now, two seaplane bases, one state-owned, and the community-owned airport welcome Annette Island's flying visitors.

RIGHT: *As an established Native reservation, Annette Island is not subject to state or federal control. Instead, the Metlakatla Indian Community maintains its own court system and staff of police officers. Visitors are welcome on the island, but are expected to abide by local tribal law. (Jerry Jordan)*

LOWER RIGHT: *Nature lovers enjoy hiking on the island's trails, like this one near Point Davison, that wind through acres of old-growth forests on the 7.8-square-mile island. (Jerry Jordan)*

For those traveling by boat, the only other way to reach the island, two marine ways and two small boat harbors along with a dock and barge ramp are available. Regular flights from charter companies out of Ketchikan service travelers to Metlakatla year-round, while the Alaska Marine Highway System ferry operates from spring through fall.

New tourism efforts assure visitors plenty of entertainment and things to see; however, those wishing to stay on the island for extended periods must first obtain permission from Metlakatla Indian Community. Services available in town include lodging, general merchandise stores, automobile repair and restaurants.

Every day during the summer, planeloads of tour groups visit Metlakatla and spend the entire day on a guided adventure around the island. Fourth Generation, a Tsimshian dance troupe of approximately 60 children and adults, performs daily at the longhouse. After the performance, everyone feasts at the Salmon Bake next door, then it's off for a tour of the packing company, Father Duncan's Cottage and Museum, and other attractions around the island.

Founder's Day, Aug. 7, commemorates William Duncan and his followers' arrival to the island in 1887. Tribal dances, button blanket creation and a potlatch help to celebrate this most important anniversary. On this day most businesses shut down so that everyone can take part in the fun.

A new project has become the talk of the town and a much anticipated event for the entire island. In May 1997, John

Pearson, tourism coordinator for Metlakatla, and local artist Wayne Hewson traveled to a Smithsonian Institution storage warehouse in Maryland to open crates containing an original Tsimshian house front from Fort Simpson. The house front was taken from Fort Simpson 122 years ago and has been in storage since 1876. Pearson and Hewson plan to restore it, bring it back to Metlakatla and place it on display inside the Tsimshian longhouse by summer 1998. Pearson described the house front as having 38 feet of imagery that depicts an ancient Tsimshian legend about two killer whales and the chief of the sea. It is the only complete house front of its kind known to exist.

Another exciting addition to Annette Island is a road from Metlakatla to Waldon Point, due to be finished in 2000. Built by the National Guard with federal funds, the road will link to a new ferry shuttle system from Revillagigedo Island, similar to the one that currently runs from Metlakatla to Ketchikan. Depending on the exact locations of the ferry terminals, the ride between islands should be 18 to 35 minutes long compared to the two-hour ride on the current ferry. ∎

BELOW LEFT: *Local artist Wayne Hewson decorated Metlakatla's tribal longhouse with traditional Tsimshian designs. Residents use the longhouse for tribal events, gatherings and educational programs. (Jerry Jordan)*

BELOW: *Inside the longhouse, Tsimshian dancers perform daily in traditional Native attire for tourists and locals. (Jerry Jordan)*

ABOVE: *Seaweed collected from island beaches makes up a large portion of the Tsimshian's subsistence diet. Locals also harvest fish, waterfowl and clams to supplement their incomes. (Jerry Jordan)*

RIGHT: *Annette Island Packing Co. cannery in Metlakatla has been in operation since 1890, and is supplied by the community's floating fish traps and commercial fishing fleet. In 1971, the company added a cold storage plant. (Jerry Jordan)*

Hyder

By Penny Rennick

The first thing that visitors notice when approaching Hyder by water is that a line appears to have been shaved up one of the mountainsides. From down Portland Canal, a crew member from the ferry *Aurora* announces that the international border is visible off the port bow. And the shaved swath is actually a clear-cut that marks the Alaska-Canada border, a line that does not stop until it reaches the Arctic Ocean.

Next, visitors notice that Hyder is small, isolated and is inhabited by some mighty independent folks.

"We don't pay any taxes here," is the first thing that guide Rita Lambert tells me as we pull out of the Grand View Inn parking area for a tour of Hyder and neighboring Stewart, B.C. No sales tax, no property tax, no local tax of any kind. Only the federal income tax has made its way to Hyder. The manager of the Grand View, Phyllis Tschakert, had recommended Rita. She arrived promptly in her older car, willing to take me wherever I wanted to go and to answer questions about the town and about herself. Since visitors need a vehicle to see much of the area, Rita saw a niche and filled it. Her fees are paid in cash.

Hyder doesn't have a bank, doesn't have a school either, or a U.S. area code for the phone system. Or medical care. The bank is in Stewart, and Canadian money works just as well as American in Hyder. The hospital is in Stewart. Schoolchildren are bused to Stewart where the state of Alaska pays to have them educated. The state pays the Canadian school district a set fee based on what it costs to educate a child in Stewart. For the 1995-1996 term, the amount was a tad more than $92,800 U.S. for 18 students. In addition, the state paid $47,000 for a teacher to teach American and Alaska history, government and social studies. Otherwise, the American children are taught the same subjects as the Canadians. A private contractor is paid $124 per day during the current term to transport the students to school.

Caroline Gutierrez, administrative assistant for the Hyder Community Association and a 21-year resident of the community, explains the general attitude toward taxes. Says Caroline, taxes would "forever ruin the way of life of Hyder." No taxes

FACING PAGE: *The town of Hyder looks to tourism to underpin its future economy. Mining, which had been the major economic force in the community for many decades, has petered out in the area. (Don Cornelius)*

Hyder in its heyday consisted of several rows of buildings built on 8- to 10-foot pilings over the tidal flats at the head of Portland Canal. The remainder of the buildings spilled over onto solid ground. About 300 people lived in the mining community at that time, more than three times the number that live there now. (Alaska Postcards Collection, Alaska State Library, Photo No. PCA 145-34-7)

means it doesn't cost anything to own land in Hyder. There isn't much land for sale, and what little there is is expensive. Much of the land is owned by people who have never been to Hyder, even the second generation of people who have never been to Hyder.

A small population is OK by many of the town's longtime residents. Ron Thomas came to Hyder in spring 1970 after living a few years in Ketchikan. When asked when is the best time to be in Hyder, Ron responds, "When nobody is here." That would be winter, when snow slides can bring vehicle and air traffic to a halt and the ferries don't run.

The gold rush put Hyder on the map. Until recent years, mining has kept it there, tucked in the out-of-the-way, extreme eastern corner of Alaska, a 10-hour, every-other-week ferry ride down Revilla Channel and up Portland Canal from Ketchikan. Or a 45-minute flight over Misty Fiords National Monument and Tongass National Forest from Ketchikan, weather permitting. The easiest way to get there is to go through Canada, on a paved, 40-mile spur off the Cassiar Highway.

Visitors arriving by road first hit Stewart, the area service center, about 1,000 residents strong, with a neatly laid out townsite, a recognizable town center and the air of a middle-aged matron. Its neighbor, Hyder, about three miles farther and

RIGHT: *The Steller's jay was the first bird species described for Alaska when it was spotted by George Steller, who accompanied Vitus Bering on his 1741 voyage to Alaska. (Sharon Brosamle)*

BELOW RIGHT: *One of the few businesses to remain open year-round, the Border Cafe is at times the busiest place in town. (Penny Rennick)*

an international boundary away, can muster fewer than 100 year-round residents and comes across as a wayward stepchild who does things his own way.

As far as is known, the Nass Indians from British Columbia's interior first traveled through this region on hunting and food-gathering forays and while escaping from Haida warriors from the coast. In 1896 the U.S. Army Corps of Engineers sent Capt. D.D. Gaillard to explore upper Portland Canal. A stone store-house, built by Gaillard's crew and the oldest masonry building in Alaska, awaits visitors who disembark from the ferry and walk into town.

By 1898, prospectors had arrived at the head of the 90-mile-long canal aboard the *Discovery* on its run north from Seattle. Among the initial wave of gold-seekers were "Pap" Stewart and John E. Stark. In 1902, brothers Robert M. and John W. Stewart arrived. The brothers laid out a townsite near the Bear River and formed the Stewart Land Co. Ltd. to represent their interests. Robert became the first postmaster and chose his last name as the official designation for the town in 1905.

Meanwhile, Daniel and Andrew Lindeborg prospected in western Alaska before finding their way to the mouth of the Salmon River where they set up a homestead in the early years of the 20th century. This site grew into the future town of Hyder, which was known as Portland City until U.S. postal officials complained that there were too many communities named "Portland" and selected the name "Hyder" to honor Canadian mining engineer Frederick B. Hyder.

Both towns were built on pilings over the tidal flats and spilled over onto adjacent land. While there is some flat ground

where the Salmon and Bear rivers have carved out their flood-plain, the steep Reverdy Mountains split the two valleys and separate the communities. The international boundary in this area runs along these mountains. Prospectors had claims on creeks flowing into both drainages, but as things turned out, production on the Canadian side surpassed that on the American. Mining expanded at a steady but low-key level during the early years, but shipping the ore down Portland Canal and resupplying the towns by boat hindered development.

It wasn't long before entrepreneurs and developers saw an opportunity. For some, rail was the answer. In 1910, Mackenzie, Mann and Co., expanding on the scope of an earlier railway charter issued to the Portland Canal Short Line, dreamed of building a rail link from tidewater several hundred miles east to the Peace River agricultural belt of northern Alberta. The company officially opened its line on June 17, 1911, with a run to Wards Pass, the railhead. Stewart mushroomed and Hyder sputtered to life as word spread of a possible boomtown. In

Stewart, H.C. Morris opened a branch of the Canadian Bank of Commerce in makeshift quarters in another store. A case of hobnailed boots covered with wrapping paper was his counter, his chair a case of condensed milk.

While Mackenzie, Mann promoted their rail line, the Grand Trunk Pacific Mail sent its steamer *Prince Rupert* to begin weekly service between the head of the canal and Prince Rupert, Vancouver, Victoria and Seattle.

A road was built up the Salmon River valley, a bridge was built over the Salmon River and a covered bridge was put in to provide access to the West Fork of Texas Creek and ultimately to

BELOW LEFT: *The road up the Salmon River valley eventually climbs the east side, providing spectacular views of Canada's Salmon Glacier. (Patrick Windsor)*

BELOW: *Carl Bradford staffs the Hyder Museum, which displays historical photos, books and items from early-day life in the tiny settlement. The museum also has records of several of the newspapers that reported events in Hyder and neighboring Stewart. (Penny Rennick)*

Passengers and crew help unload a floatplane at the Hyder dock. Residents of Hyder order many of their daily supplies in Ketchikan and the items are brought over by floatplane. (Penny Rennick)

Chickamin Glacier. Texas Creek Bridge No. 393 was the last standing covered bridge in Alaska, a 122-foot, 6-inch wood truss bridge built in 1927 to provide access to the Chickamin Mining District. The bridge was not maintained and gradually deteriorated until it collapsed in March 1979.

The mineral finds with the best potential still lay in Canada, but could only be reached by going through Hyder and up the Salmon River valley back into Canada. When the big Premier Mine began producing just after World War I, Hyder looked to a rosy future. William McDougal and Norman Hutchings started a bunkhouse at Hyder in August 1919. That same month W.J. Crawford brought his freighting business to the Salmon River valley. Hyder's independent spirit reached the boiling point in 1920 when locals tarred and feathered Jack Sutherland, organizer for the Alaska Labor Union, who was accused of

violating the northern code. On July 3, 1921, the Anyox All Star baseball team from Portland Inlet, south of Portland Canal in Canadian territory, arrived at Hyder to participate in the festivities of the year's biggest holiday. The main section of the town at that time was built on pilings 8 to 10 feet above the tidal flats. According to Ozzie Hutchings, longtime resident of the area, about 300 people lived in Hyder. He described the community that rollicking holiday: "Then the gateway to all of the mining camps up the Salmon River, the town was wide open, 24 hours a day." But all the silver and gold of the Premier Mine couldn't ease the calamities faced by those frontier festivities. The baseball games were played on the tidal flats. The first game of the day, played in the morning, "was curtailed when the tide came in and water covered the southern portion of the field with outfielders standing in water to their knees...."

In 1925, a 60-ton mill to concentrate gold-silver-lead ore was put in at the Riverside Mine, also in the Salmon River valley. More than 200 tons of concentrate left the mine the following year. A wharf was built two-thirds of a mile out into Portland Canal, providing deep water access to Hyder and Stewart year-round. Steamships offered service from Vancouver, and from Prince Rupert 135 miles away, and weekly mailboats called from Ketchikan 155 miles distant. Mining in one form or another kept the region's economy going, but when the Granduc copper mine closed in the early 1980s, the big lode mines grew silent.

ABOVE LEFT: *A winter wren forages for insects along a beach. Birdwatchers have discovered that Hyder offers one of the few opportunities in Alaska to see species more common farther south. (Don Cornelius)*

LEFT: *Downtown Hyder sports a frontier appearance. The banner spanning the road at the end of the street welcomes visitors to the town. The road to Stewart goes around the rock bluff to the left beyond the banner. (Don Pitcher)*

The ferry Aurora *unloads vehicles at the dock located between Hyder, Alaska, and Stewart, B.C. Ahead of the vessel's bow lies Stewart; Hyder (not visible) is behind and to the left. It takes 10 hours to make the run from Ketchikan south to Dixon Entrance and up Portland Canal to the dock. (Penny Rennick)*

The mining that underpinned Hyder's former growth has petered out. And for a time it looked like Hyder would do the same, when it had a population of only about 30 in the 1950s. Townfolks now say that there basically is no mining in the area. Westmin Resources, Ltd., which has the Premier Mine, had a handful of employees in the valley in winter 1996-1997. Caroline Gutierrez says that there are always prospectors combing the streams, looking for El Dorado. But she says townsfolk don't get excited about mining news because they've been disappointed too many times by reputed booms that turn bust.

Then why do people live in Hyder? "People move to Hyder because they want out of wherever they are," says Caroline. "There are more people than jobs, so there's welfare and lots of unemployment." Being a bartender was the only full-time, year-round job until recently. Now there are no full-time, year-round jobs. In addition to running the office for Hyder Community Association, Caroline sells beads to tourists and is known as the "bead lady." Some businesses close in the winter; those that remain open do remodeling and repair projects in the quiet off-season. Gary Benedict, who owns many businesses in Hyder including the Sealaska Hotel, Beneducci's Restaurant — for which 1980s advertisements boast "For Your Tax-free Dining Pleasure" — and two RV parks, spends summers in town and winters in Hawaii. The Border Cafe remains open, as does Canal Trading, Dean's Grocery and Mom's This & That Shop, a gift store.

Hyder's remote location and small population hasn't prevented missionaries from taking hold here. One church operates in town with several more in Stewart.

On July 3, 1995, fire destroyed the community hall, taking with it the post office, fire hall and library. What could be salvaged or collected for the library is stored in a tiny, but intriguing, museum on Main Street staffed by Carl Bradford. Historical photos, exhibits and books provide a glimpse of early Hyder. In keeping with the town's philosophy of no taxes, admission to the museum is free. As Caroline says, people charge too much for too many things, and "it's nice to have something free." A new community hall is scheduled to open in 1997, providing space for the community association, the library and newly acquired pumper and tanker fire trucks, 1970-1973 vintage.

Even with its troubles, the town keeps going and the tourists, the economic foundation of the town, keep coming. The state pays Hyder Community Association to keep the road open from the border near Stewart into Hyder; and Westmin, the Canadian mining firm, pays the association to keep the road open north of Hyder up the Salmon River valley to the border, a distance of 11 miles. Westmin's Premier Mine is four miles beyond the border.

Most tourists come to see the bears that feed near the road, munching on greenery in early summer and on runs of chum and pink salmon from mid-July to the end of August. The chum runs in the Salmon River drainage are particularly large and attract brown and black bears. Misty Fiords National Monument staff manage the natural resources of the drainage for the U.S. Forest Service and are striving to craft a solid plan to handle the increasing number of tourists and protect the bears. Any plan will have to deal with the proximity of bears and people along Salmon River Road. The forest service has constructed a boardwalk along Fish Creek, a few miles up valley from Hyder. But the creek parallels the road for a bit before flowing under the road and downstream by the boardwalk. And the bears are

Kayakers raft up and drift with the tide while eating lunch in Misty Fiords' Rudyerd Bay. Tongass National Forest and its Misty Fiords National Monument separate Hyder from Ketchikan and other coastal communities in southern Southeast. (Jon R. Nickles)

just as willing to fish by the road as by the boardwalk. Monument staff would like to limit visitation to prevent bear/people mishaps, but the road is a state highway open to all. And some people adopt unwise behavior when they are close to bears.

Beyond the bear-viewing area, the road climbs the east side of the Salmon River valley, passes abandoned mines, remnants of an old tramway and crosses back into Canada. Densely forested, steep mountainsides rise to the east. To the west the vista sweeps over and down in memorable images of Salmon Glacier, source of the Salmon River.

This area offers fine snow machining in winter. In summer visitor interest focuses on the bears, the glacier, fishing and hiking. Lengthy hiking trails are uncommon in the vertical world of Southeast Alaska. Monument staff would like to expand the Titan Trail and perhaps connect it with a trail on the Canadian side that would create a 12-mile route. An old mule trail, the Titan begins about a quarter-mile beyond the bear-watching area, climbs about five miles through spruce, crosses streams, old avalanche chutes filled with large ferns, opens onto vistas of the Salmon River drainage and ends at the old Titan Mine. Bears use the trail early morning and evening so hikers should pick their time carefully and make noise.

Because of its position as the southernmost place on the mainland of Southeast that is accessible by road, the Hyder area also attracts birdwatchers who come seeking species like the American redstart, black swift and magnolia warbler that are difficult to find in the rest of Alaska.

Just as in the past, Hyder's big holiday is the combined celebration of Independence Days for Canada and the United States from July 1 through July 4 and sometimes beyond. A second visitor draw is the Stewart Hyder International Rodeo held the second weekend in June with dances and rodeo competition.

So what's in store for Hyder, the "Friendliest Ghost Town in Alaska"? When asked if there are plans for expansion in Hyder, Caroline says emphatically, "I hope not." Perhaps Ron Thomas captured the essence of Hyder most succinctly: It's the best of all possible worlds, he says, "No taxes and nearby medical care." ∎

Bibliography

Ackerman, Robert E. "Earliest Stone Industries of the North Pacific Coast of North America." *Arctic Anthropology*, Vol. 29, No. 2, pp. 18-27. 1992.

—, Kenneth C. Reid, James D. Gallison and Mark E. Roe. "Archaeology of Heceta Island: A Survey of 16 Timber Harvest Units in the Tongass National Forest, Southeastern Alaska," Project Report Number 3. Pullman, Wash.: Center for Northwest Anthropology, Washington State University, 1985.

Alaska Department of Community & Regional Affairs. *Community Profile: Metlakatla*. Juneau: State of Alaska, Municipal & Regional Assistance Division, 1996.

Allen, June. "McRae Acted in First Film Here," *Ketchikan Daily News*, Oct. 23, 1990.

Balcom, Mary. *Ghost Towns of Alaska*. Chicago: Adams Press, 1965.

Boyce, David, Curator. North Pacific Cannery Museum: Port Edward, British Columbia, pers. com., March 1996.

Brew, D. A., G. R. Himmelberg, R. A. Loney and A. B. Ford. "Distribution and characteristics of metamorphic belts in the south-eastern Alaska part of the North American cordillera." *Journal of Metamorphic Geology*, Vol. 10, pp. 465-482. 1992a.

—, J. D. Lawrence and S. D. Ludington. "The study of the undiscovered mineral resources of the Tongass National Forest and adjacent lands, southeastern Alaska." In: *Nonrenewable Resources*. Oxford Univ. Press, Vol. 1, No. 4, pp. 303-322. 1992.

Buddington, A.F. *Geology of Hyder and Vicinity Southeastern Alaska*. U.S. Geological Survey Bulletin 807. Washington D.C.: Department of the Interior, 1929.

Case, David S. *Alaska Natives and American Laws*. Fairbanks, Alaska: University of Alaska Press, 1984.

Chew, Ron, Director and Ruth Vincent, Curator. Wing Luke Asian Museum, Seattle. pers. com., March 1996.

Davis, Stanley D.. "Prehistory of Southeastern Alaska": In Wayne Suttles, ed. *Handbook of North American Indians*, Vol. 7, Northwest Coast. Washington, D. C.: Smithsonian Institution, 1990.

DeArmond, R.N.*Southeast Alaska: Names on the Chart and How They Got There*. Juneau: Commercial Art, Inc. 1989.

Dixon, E. James. *Quest for the Origins of the First Americans*, Albuquerque: University of New Mexico Press, 1993.

Easton, N. Alexander. "Mal de Mer above Terra Incognita, or, 'What Ails the Coastal Migration Theory?'," *Arctic Anthropology* Vol. 29, No. 2, pp. 28-42, 1992.

Engstrom, D. R., B. C. S. Hansen and H. E. Wright Jr. "A Possible Younger Dryas Record in Southeastern Alaska." *Science*, Vol. 250, pp. 1383-1385, 1990.

Eppenbach, Sarah. *Alaska's Southeast*. Chester, Conn.: The Globe Pequot Press, 1991.

Fedje, Daryl W., Joanne B. McSporran and Andrew R. Mason. "Early Holocene Archaeology and Paleoecology at the Arrow Creek Sites in Gwaii Haanas." *Arctic Anthropology*, Vol. 33, No. 1, pp. 116-142, 1996.

Fladmark, Knut R. "Possible Early Human Occupations of the Queen Charlotte Islands, British Columbia," *Canadian Journal of Archaeology*, Vol. 14, pp. 183-197, 1990.

Gehrels, George E. and Henry C. Berg. "Geology of Southeastern Alaska": In: Plafker, G., and Berg. H.C., eds., *The Geology of North America*, Vol. G-1, The Geology of Alaska. Boulder, Colo.: The Geological Society of America, pp.451-467, 1994.

Hansen, Barbra C. S. and Daniel R. Engstrom. "Vegetation History of Pleasant Island, Southeastern Alaska, since 13,000 yr. B. P." *Quaternary Research*, No. 46, pp. 161-175, 1996.

Heaton, Timothy H., Sandra L. Talbot and Gerald F. Shields. "An Ice Age Refugium for Large Mammals in the Alexander Archipelago, Southeastern Alaska," *Quaternary Research*, No. 46, pp 186-192, 1996.

Henning, Robert, ed. *Southeast: Alaska's Panhandle. ALASKA GEOGRAPHIC®*, Vol. 5, No. 2. Anchorage: Alaska Geographic Society, 1978.

Inventory of the Alaska Packers Association Records, 1970.

Johanson, Sixten. "The Greenland Sailed Away." *The Alaska Sportsman*, June 1951.

Jones, Nikki Murray, ed. *1996 Prince of Wales Island Guide*. Ketchikan: Pioneer Printing Co. Inc., 1996.

Josenhans, Heiner W., Daryl W. Fedje, Kim W. Conway and J. Vaughn Barrie. "Post Glacial sea levels on the Western Canadian continental shelf: evidence for rapid change, extensive subaerial exposure, and early human habitation." *Marine Geology*, 125, pp. 73-94, 1995.

Ketchikan Alaska Chronicle, May 15, June 13, June 19, July 3, July 7, July 9, July 19, July 21, July 22, July 23, August 5, August 7, November 8, 1930.

Kutchin, M., Special Agent. *Report on the Salmon Fisheries of Alaska, 1902*. Washington D.C.: U.S. Government Printing Office, 1903.

Mann, Daniel, H. "Wisconsin and Holocene Glaciation of Southeast Alaska." In: T.D. Hamilton, K.M. Reed and R.M. Thorson, eds. *Glaciation in Alaska — The Geologic Record*. Anchorage: Alaska Geological Society, pp. 237-265, 1986.

McCunn, Ruthanne Lum. *Chinese American Portraits*. San Francisco: Chronicle Books, 1988.

Mobley, Charles M. "Holocene Sea Levels in Southeast Alaska: Preliminary Results." *Arctic*, Vol. 41, No. 4, pp. 261-266, 1988.

Moss, Madonna L. "Relationships Between Maritime Cultures of Southern Alaska: Rethinking Culture Area Boundaries," *Arctic Anthropology*, Vol. 29, No. 2, pp. 5-17, 1992.

— and Jon M. Erlandson. "Reflections on North American Pacific Coast Prehistory," *Journal of World Prehistory*, Vol. 9, No. 1, pp. 1-45, 1995.

Muir, John. *Travels in Alaska*. Boston: Houghton-Mifflin, 1915.

Okada, H., A. Okada, K. Yajima, W. Olson, M. Sugita, N. Shianosaki, S. Okino, K. Yoshida, and H. Kaneko. *Heceta Island, Southeastern Alaska: Anthropological Survey in 1989 and 1990*. Sapporo, Japan: Department of Behavioral Science, Hokkaido University, 1992.

Okada, H., A. Okada, Y. Kotani, K. Yajima, W.M. Olson, T. Nishimoto, and S. Okino. *Heceta Island, Southeastern Alaska: Anthropological Survey in 1987*. Sapporo, Japan: Department of Behavioral Science, Hokkaido University, 1989.

Olson, Wallace M. "A Prehistory of Southeast Alaska," *ALASKA GEOGRAPHIC®*, Vol. 21, No. 4. Anchorage: Alaska Geographic Society, 1994.

Orth, Donald. *Dictionary of Alaska Place Names*. Washington D.C.: United States Goverment Printing Office, 1967.

Pewe, Troy L. "Quaternary Geology of Alaska," *U.S. Geological Survey Professional Paper 835*. Washington D.C., U.S. Geological Survey, 1983.

Pielou, E. C. *After the Ice Age, The Return of Life to Glaciated North America*. Chicago: University of Chicago Press, 1991.

Putnam, David E. and Terence Fifield. "Estuarine Archaeology and Holocene Sea-Level Change on Prince of Wales Island, Alaska." In. Proceedings of "Hidden Dimensions": the Cultural Significance of Wetland Archaeology, Vancouver, British Columbia, Canada, April 1995, (In press).

Report on Population and Resources of Alaska at the Eleventh Census, 1890. Washington, D.C.: U.S. Government Printing Office, 1893.

Roppel, Patricia. *An Historical Guide to Revillagegedo and Gravina Islands*. Wrangell, Alaska: Farwest Research, 1995.

—. "Loring," *The Alaska Journal*, Vol. 5, No. 3, pp. 168-178. Juneau: Alaska Northwest Publishing Co., 1975.

—. *Southeast Alaska, A Pictorial History*. Norfolk VA.: The Donning Co., 1983.

Shields, Irene, Cape Fox Corp., pers. com. April 1995.

Smith, Mary, and Louise Brinck Harrington. *I Never Did Mind the Rain*. Ketchikan: Friends of Ketchikan Public Library, 1995.

Streveler, Greg. *The Natural History of Gustavus*. Juneau: Greg Streveler, 1996.

—, Richard Carstensen and Gretchen Bishop. *A Naturalist's Look at Southeast Alaska*. Juneau: Discovery Foundation, 1993.

Twenhofel, William S. "Recent Shore-line Changes Along the Pacific Coast of Alaska." *American Journal of Science*, Vol. 250, pp. 523-548, 1952.

Watkins, Alison. "Metlakatla's Waldon Point work to begin in summer," *Ketchikan Daily News*, Jan. 11-12, 1997.

Workman, William. "The First of the Last: Pioneer Human Settlers on the Last Frontier," *ALASKA GEOGRAPHIC®*, Vol. 21, No. 4. Anchorage: Alaska Geographic Society, 1994. ∎

(Penny Rennick)

Index

ALASKA GEOGRAPHIC® Back Issues

The North Slope, Vol. 1, No. 1. Out of print.

One Man's Wilderness, Vol. 1, No. 2. Out of print.

Admiralty...Island in Contention, Vol. 1, No. 3. $19.95.

Fisheries of the North Pacific, Vol. 1, No. 4. Out of print.

Alaska-Yukon Wild Flowers, Vol. 2, No. 1. Out of print.

Richard Harrington's Yukon, Vol. 2, No. 2. Out of print.

Prince William Sound, Vol. 2, No. 3. Out of print.

Yakutat: The Turbulent Crescent, Vol. 2, No. 4. Out of print.

Glacier Bay: Old Ice, New Land, Vol. 3, No. 1. Out of print.

The Land: Eye of the Storm, Vol. 3, No. 2. Out of print.

Richard Harrington's Antarctic, Vol. 3, No. 3. $19.95.

The Silver Years, Vol. 3, No. 4. $19.95.

Alaska's Volcanoes, Vol. 4, No. 1. Out of print.

The Brooks Range, Vol. 4, No. 2. Out of print.

Kodiak: Island of Change, Vol. 4, No. 3. Out of print.

Wilderness Proposals, Vol. 4, No. 4. Out of print.

Cook Inlet Country, Vol. 5, No. 1. Out of print.

Southeast: Alaska's Panhandle, Vol. 5, No. 2. Out of print.

Bristol Bay Basin, Vol. 5, No. 3. Out of print.

Alaska Whales and Whaling, Vol. 5, No. 4. $19.95.

Yukon-Kuskokwim Delta, Vol. 6, No. 1. Out of print.

Aurora Borealis, Vol. 6, No. 2. $19.95.

Alaska's Native People, Vol. 6, No. 3. $24.95. Out of print.

The Stikine River, Vol. 6, No. 4. $19.95.

Alaska's Great Interior, Vol. 7, No. 1. $19.95.

Photographic Geography of Alaska, Vol. 7, No. 2. Out of print.

The Aleutians, Vol. 7, No. 3. Out of print.

Klondike Lost, Vol. 7, No. 4. Out of print.

Wrangell-Saint Elias, Vol. 8, No. 1. Out of print.

Alaska Mammals, Vol. 8, No. 2. Out of print.

The Kotzebue Basin, Vol. 8, No. 3. Out of print.

Alaska National Interest Lands, Vol. 8, No. 4. $19.95.

Alaska's Glaciers, Vol. 9, No. 1. Revised 1993. $19.95.

Sitka and Its Ocean/Island World, Vol. 9, No. 2. Out of print.

Islands of the Seals: The Pribilofs, Vol. 9, No. 3. $19.95.

Alaska's Oil/Gas & Minerals Industry, Vol. 9, No. 4. $19.95.

Adventure Roads North, Vol. 10, No. 1. $19.95.

Anchorage and the Cook Inlet Basin, Vol. 10, No. 2. $19.95.

Alaska's Salmon Fisheries, Vol. 10, No. 3. $19.95.

Up the Koyukuk, Vol. 10, No. 4. $19.95.

Nome: City of the Golden Beaches, Vol. 11, No. 1. $19.95.

Alaska's Farms and Gardens, Vol. 11, No. 2. $19.95.

Chilkat River Valley, Vol. 11, No. 3. $19.95.

Alaska Steam, Vol. 11, No. 4. $19.95.

Northwest Territories, Vol. 12, No. 1. $19.95.

Alaska's Forest Resources, Vol. 12, No. 2. $19.95.

Alaska Native Arts and Crafts, Vol. 12, No. 3. $24.95.

Our Arctic Year, Vol. 12, No. 4. $19.95.

Where Mountains Meet the Sea, Vol. 13, No. 1. $19.95.

Backcountry Alaska, Vol. 13, No. 2. $19.95.

British Columbia's Coast, Vol. 13, No. 3. $19.95.

Lake Clark/Lake Iliamna, Vol. 13, No. 4. Out of print.

Dogs of the North, Vol. 14, No. 1. $19.95.

South/Southeast Alaska, Vol. 14, No. 2. Out of print.

Alaska's Seward Peninsula, Vol. 14, No. 3. $19.95.

The Upper Yukon Basin, Vol. 14, No. 4. $19.95.

Glacier Bay: Icy Wilderness, Vol. 15, No. 1. Out of print.

Dawson City, Vol. 15, No. 2. $19.95.

Denali, Vol. 15, No. 3. $19.95.

The Kuskokwim River, Vol. 15, No. 4. $19.95.

Katmai Country, Vol. 16, No. 1. $19.95.

North Slope Now, Vol. 16, No. 2. $19.95.

The Tanana Basin, Vol. 16, No. 3. $19.95.

The Copper Trail, Vol. 16, No. 4. $19.95.

The Nushagak Basin, Vol. 17, No. 1. $19.95.

Juneau, Vol. 17, No. 2. Out of print.

The Middle Yukon River, Vol. 17, No. 3. $19.95.

The Lower Yukon River, Vol. 17, No. 4. $19.95.

Alaska's Weather, Vol. 18, No. 1. $19.95.

Alaska's Volcanoes, Vol. 18, No. 2. $19.95.

Admiralty Island: Fortress of Bears, Vol. 18, No. 3. $19.95.

Unalaska/Dutch Harbor, Vol. 18, No. 4. $19.95.

Skagway: A Legacy of Gold, Vol. 19, No. 1. $19.95.

ALASKA: The Great Land, Vol. 19, No. 2. $19.95.

Kodiak, Vol. 19, No. 3. $19.95.

Alaska's Railroads, Vol. 19, No. 4. $19.95.

Prince William Sound, Vol. 20, No. 1. $19.95.

Southeast Alaska, Vol. 20, No. 2. $19.95.

Arctic National Wildlife Refuge, Vol. 20, No. 3. $19.95.

Alaska's Bears, Vol. 20, No. 4. $19.95.

The Alaska Peninsula, Vol. 21, No. 1. $19.95.

The Kenai Peninsula, Vol. 21, No. 2. $19.95.

People of Alaska, Vol. 21, No. 3. $19.95.

Prehistoric Alaska, Vol. 21, No. 4. $19.95.

Fairbanks, Vol. 22, No. 1. $19.95.

The Aleutian Islands, Vol. 22, No. 2. $19.95.

Rich Earth: Alaska's Mineral Industry, Vol. 22, No. 3. $19.95.

World War II in Alaska, Vol. 22, No. 4. $19.95.

Anchorage, Vol. 23, No. 1. $21.95.

Native Cultures in Alaska, Vol. 23, No. 2. $19.95.

The Brooks Range, Vol. 23, No. 3. $19.95.

Moose, Caribou and Muskox, Vol. 23, No. 4. $19.95.

PRICES AND AVAILABILITY SUBJECT TO CHANGE

Membership in The Alaska Geographic Society includes a subscription to *ALASKA GEOGRAPHIC*®, the Society's colorful, award-winning quarterly.

Call or write for current membership rates or to request a free catalog. *ALASKA GEOGRAPHIC*® back issues are also available (see above list). **NOTE:** This list was current in mid-1997. If more than a year or two have elapsed since that time, please contact us before ordering to check prices and availability of specific back issues.

When ordering back issues please add $2 postage/handling per book for Book Rate; $4 each for Priority Mail. Inquire for non-U.S. postage rates. To order send check or money order (U.S. funds) or VISA/MasterCard information (including expiration date and your phone number) with list of titles desired to:

ALASKA GEOGRAPHIC.
P.O. Box 93370 • Anchorage, AK 99509-3370
Phone: (907) 562-0164 • Fax (907) 562-0479

NEXT ISSUE:

The Golden Gamble, Vol. 24, No. 2.

The gold rushes of the late 19th and early 20th centuries produced more than gold. They spurred development of infrastructure in the Far North, and did much to spike a West Coast economy that had languished during the 1890s. As Alaska and Canada's Yukon Territory celebrate the centennial of the gold rush, *ALASKA GEOGRAPHIC*® joins the commemoration with an issue on the golden gamble and its effect on the country's West Coast from California to Alaska. To members mid-1997.